"This book is a great resource for school leaders interested in better understanding the role of the superintendent. It will help educational leaders improve professional practice."—**Sarah A. Hall**, PhD, associate professor, Ashland University, Ohio

"The authors correctly underscore the importance of the superintendent's role as instructional leader. Their work is spot on, informative, illuminating, and will certainly serve as an important resource for both new and experienced superintendents."—**Elaine Pinckney**, superintendent, Chittenden South Supervisory Union, Shelburne, Vermont

"This book provides a comprehensive review of the evolution of the superintendency. It's a critical read for current superintendents, those working with superintendents, and those who aspire to this critical educational leadership position."—**Jason E. Leahy**, Illinois Principals' Association, PA executive director, Springfield, Illinois

"The authors provide an excellent basis for understanding the role of the superintendent. I'm confident that this book will provide a positive contribution to education through its balance between research-based competencies and real world case study scenarios."—**Howard C. Carlson**, EdD, superintendent, Wickenburg Unified School District, Wickenburg, Arizona

"The superintendent as 'instructional leader' has been the most profound role expectation and force in the profession over the past five years. These experienced administrators present effective, field-tested strategies that make the connection between superintendent leadership and student achievement. A real game changer."—**Dr. Joseph M. Porto**, JMP Consulting, LTD., retired superintendent, Avoka District 37, Wilmette, Illinois

"I highly recommend this book for any sitting school district leader and for those aspiring to be highly effective school superintendents in the future."—**David R. Schuler**, PhD, superintendent of schools, Township High School District 214; AASA 2015–2016 president

"The role of the superintendent as an instructional leader is critical to the future of education and this book is a practical and understandable resource. I highly recommend this book."—**Dr. Rosarie P. Jean**, New York City Department of Education, Bronx, New York

"The authors provide an excellent basis for understanding the role of the superintendent. I'm confident that this book will provide a positive contribution to the field of education."—**Bill Robertson**, EdD, superintendent of schools

"As the school superintendency is by far one of the most complex positions, the authors have truly captured the essence of the job in a well written resource. I highly recommend for any current or future superintendent."—**S. Dallas Dance**, superintendent, Baltimore County Public Schools

"The authors have written a book addressing superintendent competencies to meet community, academic, and cultural needs through a new mindset. This work creates a new vision of superintendent leadership that is intentional and inclusive."—**Ron Warwick**, EdD, professor of leadership, Concordia University Chicago

"This book not only puts the work of the superintendency in a clear contextual framework but offers concrete and meaningful steps to take for district and school improvement. The authors highlight notable pitfalls and areas to consider with valuable solutions, case studies, and questions for mindful reflection and discussion."—**Victoria Kieffer**, PhD, principal, Townline Elementary School, Vernon Hills, Illinois

"This book offers a wealth of facts, wisdom, insights, and practical applications for twenty-first educational leaders."—**Noelle Sterne**, PhD, dissertation consultant, coach, and editor; author, *Challenges in Writing Your Dissertation*

"The authors did an excellent job explaining that the evolution of the superintendency. The role requires a highly collaborative administrative culture in which school and district leaders do more than supervise and evaluate. They teach, coach, and share the responsibility for improved teaching and learning. Well done."—**Lynette Zimmer**, EdD, superintendent, Lake Villa SD 41, Lake Villa, Illinois

"This book captures the complex role of the superintendent, blending research and practice. A great resource for current and future educational leaders."—**Tim Kilrea**, EdD, superintendent of schools, Lyons Township High School District 204, LaGrange, Illinois

"Today's discussions about leadership are really focused on change leadership and instructional leadership. If we want principals to possess and utilize these, it makes sense for superintendents to serve as role models. The authors are commended for providing a road map for superintendents to be the leading learner based on the most recent relevant research. Keep this resource handy!"—**Dr. Lyle C. Ailshie**, superintendent of schools, Kingsport City Schools, Kingsport, Tennessee

"This book provides an in-depth look at the complexities of being a school superintendent. This standards based research provides the reader keys to success in school leadership in today's society. An effective superintendent knows the importance of keeping up to date with the ever changing requirements of the district leadership position. This book does so in a way that the reader can instantaneously take these ideas for immediate improvement in district performance."—**Dr. Jim Rosborg**, McKendree University, Illinois

"This book serves as an insightful commentary for those who understand or wish to understand the changing role of the superintendent in American education. The authors focus on the realistic complexities and demands of the position while at the same time excel in framing the challenges for all school and school district leaders."—**George Zimmer**, EdD, visiting professor, Concordia University of Chicago; former superintendent, Richmond School District, Sussex, Wisconsin; former superintendent, Nippersink SD No. 2, Spring Grove and Richmond, Illinois; former superintendent, Richmond SD 13, Richmond, Illinois

"The authors provide an excellent basis for understanding the complex and complicated role of the superintendent and is an excellent read."—**Howard J. Bultinck**, PhD, professor and chair, literacy, leadership and development, Northeastern Illinois University

"This book provides a comprehensive look at the expanding roles of the superintendent in a climate of reform and accountability. The authors show how high expectations, research-based practices, and continuous improvement are as important for leaders as they are for teachers and students."—**Dr. James Rycik**, professor of education, Ashland University; editor, *American Secondary Education*

"A great resource for superintendents and district school leaders in leading school districts today. I highly recommend this book especially for aspiring school superintendents."—**Steve Webb**, PhD, superintendent, Goreville Community Unit School District #1, Illinois

"This book is an excellent reference and resource for current and aspiring superintendents. The authors have written an exceptionally insightful perspective on the many leadership dynamics that surround the public school superintendency. Their work most certainly contributes significantly to the field of educational leadership."—**Dr. Donald Hendricks**, former school superintendent for twenty-eight years; associate professor, Department of Leadership, Concordia University Chicago

"The role of the superintendent as an instructional leader is critical to the future of education and this book is a practical and understandable resource with some excellent, research based suggestions for success. I highly recommend this book."—**Ann Welk**, Round Lake School Board Member; IASB Lake Division Executive Committee Member; SEFOL Executive Board Member

"A comprehensive guide on the superintendency has been long overdue. This is a compelling and thorough text on every aspect of the superintendency. It provides an excellent basis for understanding the superintendent as instructional leader and CEO. I highly recommend this book."—**Karen Starr**, PhD, FAICD, FACEL, FACE, FIEFRC, chair of school development and leadership, Deakin University, Melbourne Burbank Campus, Australia

"*Leading with Resolve and Mastery* is a must-read for both practicing and aspiring superintendents. The authors provide not only a highly interesting, thorough history of the superintendency, but also a very readable, practical, and thorough description of both what superintendents face today, as well as how they can make a real difference in student learning and school district success."—**Thomas A. Kersten**, EdD, associate professor emeritus, Roosevelt University

"Today's superintendency dramatically differs from the role that AASA charter members fulfilled. Among the 'many hats' described by the authors, I deem that of the *learning leader* to be most critical to students' learning success. The core competencies and practical strategies in this book will prove invaluable to any superintendent who strives for excellence, and who is determined to navigate the politics to maximize student academic growth. Thus, I highly recommend *Leading with Resolve and Mastery*—it's a must-read!"—**Susan S. Bunting**, EdD, superintendent, Indian River School District, Selbyville, Delaware

Leading with
Resolve and Mastery

Other Books by the Authors
Concordia University Chicago Leadership Series

Challenging Students to Learn: How to Use Effective Leadership and Motivation Tactics (2017)

Transforming Professional Practice: A Framework for Effective Leadership (2016)

Ethics and Politics in School Leadership (2016)

Technology for Classroom and Online Learning (2015)

Grant Writing: Strategies for Scholars and Professionals (2015)

Supervision and Evaluation for Learning and Growth (2015)

The Challenge for School Leaders (2015)

The Teacher Leader: Core Competencies and Strategies for Effective Leadership (2013)

How to Finish and Defend Your Dissertation: Strategies to Complete the Professional Practice Doctorate (2013)

Leading School Change: Maximizing Resources for School Improvement (2013)

Managing Human Resources and Collective Bargaining (2013)

Resource Management for School Administrators: Optimizing Fiscal, Facility, and Human Resources (2013)

Action Research for Educators, second edition (2010)

Action Research for Educators (2005)

Discipline by Negotiation: Methods for Managing Student Behavior (2000)

Leading with Resolve and Mastery

Competency-Based Strategies for Superintendent Success

Robert K. Wilhite, Jeffrey T. Brierton,
Craig A. Schilling, and Daniel R. Tomal

Published in partnership with
The School Superintendents Association (AASA)

ROWMAN & LITTLEFIELD
Lanham • Boulder • New York • London

Published in partnership with The School Superintendents Association

Published by Rowman & Littlefield
A wholly owned subsidiary of The Rowman & Littlefield Publishing Group, Inc.
4501 Forbes Boulevard, Suite 200, Lanham, Maryland 20706
www.rowman.com

Unit A, Whitacre Mews, 26-34 Stannary Street, London SE11 4AB

British Library Cataloguing in Publication Information Available

Library of Congress Cataloging-in-Publication Data Available

ISBN: 978-1-4758-2813-9 (cloth : alk. paper)
ISBN: 978-1-4758-2814-6 (pbk. : alk. paper)
ISBN: 978-1-4758-2815-3 (electronic)

∞™ The paper used in this publication meets the minimum requirements of American National Standard for Information Sciences—Permanence of Paper for Printed Library Materials, ANSI/NISO Z39.48-1992.

Printed in the United States of America

Contents

List of Figures   xiii

Acknowledgments   xv

Foreword   xvii

Preface   xix

1 Many Hats, Many Masters   1
    The Evolving Role of the Superintendent

2 Leading with Mastery   17
    Core Competencies for Superintendents

3 Leading with Intent: A Third Way   37
    The Superintendent as Learning Leader

4 Policy and Politics   57
    The Superintendent as CEO

5 Accountability and Professional Learning   77
    The Superintendent as Supervisor and Evaluator

6 Follow Me, I Know the Way   93
    Building District Capacity for Success

7 Dollars and Sense   111
    The Superintendent as Steward

8 Seeing the Forest for the Trees   133
    Benchmarking District Performance

Appendixes

A. School Leadership Survey 149

B. Sample Professional Learning and Growth Plans 151

C. Professional Standards for Educational Leaders (PSEL) 155

Index 157

About the Authors 161

List of Figures

Figure 1.1. Three phases of development of the superintendency. 3

Figure 1.2. Factors affecting the role of the superintendent. 5

Figure 1.3. History of modern education reform legislation. 6

Figure 2.1. Twelve superintendent core competencies. 18

Figure 2.2. Knowledge and skill delivery system. 22

Figure 2.3. Diverse learner groups. 30

Figure 2.4. Integration of the professional learning community model. 31

Figure 3.1. Core competencies of school leaders. 41

Figure 3.2. Comparison of the school leader core competencies and ELCC and PSEL standards. 42

Figure 3.3. Contrast of competencies ranked by superintendents. 47

Figure 3.4. The evolution of school cultures. 48

Figure 3.5. Components of fusion leadership. 50

Figure 4.1. Framework for key work of school boards. (National School Boards Association, 2011.) 60

Figure 4.2. Sample board of education policy adoption process. 61

Figure 4.3. Theories of school board politics. 64

Figure 5.1. Qualities of an effective leadership supervision plan. 81

Figure 5.2. Qualities of an effective leadership evaluation plan.   83

Figure 5.3. Elements of a leadership professional learning and
growth plan.   89

Figure 6.1. Steps in conducting a strategic plan.   95

Figure 6.2. Components of a strategic plan.   96

Figure 6.3. Typical values of a school district leadership team.   98

Figure 6.4. Example of a strategic planning spreadsheet.   101

Figure 6.5. Steps for district-level succession planning process.   103

Figure 7.1. The relationship of fiscal integrity, student outcomes,
and efficiency and effectiveness.   112

Figure 7.2. The linkage between efficiency and effectiveness with
regard to cost and achievement.   116

Figure 7.3. Steps in the value proposition model.   119

Figure 8.1. Example of a simple dashboard report to communicate
decreasing operating reserves.   141

Figure 8.2. The relationship between the urgency and readiness
for change.   144

Figure A.1. School leadership survey.   150

Figure B.1. Sample professional learning and growth plans.   151

Acknowledgments

It is impossible to acknowledge all of those who have contributed to the development of this book. Over the collective lifetimes of the authors, we have served over 150 years in education. The many experiences, encounters, and dilemmas we have had contributed to the nature of the topics in this book. We acknowledge our families, colleagues, students, and friends, who have encouraged and provided rich ideas in the planning, writing, and release of this book.

We make special acknowledgment to the AASA, The School Superintendents Association and to Rowman & Littlefield for working with us in the publication of this book.

We invite the reader to use this book for reflection, dialogue, and critique of the present state of leadership in our schools. We challenge the reader to apply and adapt the ideas of this book to improve our classrooms and schools. Schools are the lighthouses of our communities.

Lastly, to future and present leaders, may you develop an in-depth understanding of the meaning of leadership and strive to become a more effective leader.

Foreword

Leading with Resolve and Mastery is an excellent addition to the Concordia University of Chicago Leadership Series. The role of the school superintendent today is significantly different than that of a school superintendent in years past. This publication begins by providing the historical context for the evolving role of the superintendent and accurately capturing the many, varied responsibilities of the modern superintendent.

It is incumbent for school superintendents to be able to manage the day-to-day responsibilities associated with the job. But in order to be a truly effective and successful school superintendent, I would suggest that an individual has to be able to lead and lead with mastery. The twelve superintendent leadership core competencies discussed in this book provide a road map for individuals who are interested in transcending the daily minutiae of the superintendency to truly lead their school districts and communities in a highly effective manner. The competencies are extremely compelling—from school governance to building a collaborative culture and everything in between—and provide information that high-quality school leaders need to be successful as modern-day superintendents.

I am very thankful that the authors included an entire chapter on policy and politics. Both topics are essential for school leaders to master if they want to be successful superintendents and impact positive change in their districts and communities. Understanding the importance of governance, policy, community relations, and appropriate relationships with the school board are critical concepts that the authors explore in depth. It is awesome that included in this book is a specific strategy for policy development and policy revision that is very practicable and relevant for district leaders.

To be effective in today's ever-changing global economy, school superintendents must devote time to professional growth. They also must spend time cultivating and developing human capacity within their organization. Professional development and learning activities must focus on continuous improvement and cannot be thought of as a one-size-fits-all or a one-off activity that doesn't align with the shared vision of the school district.

The format of this book is extremely impressive. Ending each chapter with a case study is a highly effective format which causes the reader to reflect and apply the objectives in each chapter in a relevant and authentic manner. This book is practical and should sit on every school superintendent's desk as a quick reference guide as we go through our work. The authors have a history of research and contributing to the profession in a positive and constructive manner and this book is no exception. I highly recommend *Leading with Resolve and Mastery* for any sitting school district leader and for those aspiring to be highly effective school superintendents in the future.

David R. Schuler, PhD
Superintendent of Schools—
Township High School District 214
AASA 2015–2016 President

Preface

School district accountability for excellence starts with the superintendent. School districts across the country continue to face a multiplicity of issues ranging from student discipline, budget constraints, high performance expectations, accountability, state and federal policies and requirements, safety, employee hiring and attrition, and teacher accountability.

The demands for high performance by all employees place increased pressures on superintendents to meet high expectations and accountability. These demands require strong instructional leadership, more rigorous superintendent and district leader training programs, demonstrated proficiency of school district leaders in teacher and administrator evaluation, an understanding of growth and change processes, and feedback that is based on relevant data-driven decision-making.

Moreover, district leaders need to have an understanding of the interrelatedness of supervision and instruction and the need to develop meaningful student growth plans for the district schools. The basis of student growth and achievement rests with sound strategic planning, high academic standards, accountability, and effective leadership. Effective school district leaders understand and are able to champion advancing the entire school district for continuous growth and improvement.

The strategies described in this book have been found successful in operating at the school district level and are especially centered on providing information in connecting the job of the superintendent with effective instruction and increased student achievement. While primarily directed toward public schools, the strategies in this book can also be effective for private elementary and secondary schools, as well as charter schools. The information and strategies are practical and useful techniques that can be used by any school district leader who desires to optimize district-level performance.

The first chapter provides a history of the role of the superintendent, the relationship of the position with stakeholders, and the basis of accountability. It describes how the role of superintendent is linked to school district effectiveness. Lastly, a summary of the key points of the chapter is provided, along with a comprehensive case study, and several exercises and discussion questions.

The foundation of chapter 2 is the research-based core competencies of the superintendent position. An outline of the core competencies of superintendents and principals as identified in a research study is presented. These competencies are measured against the standards-based competencies as seen in the Educational Leadership Constituent Council (ELCC) and the Professional Standards for Educational Leaders, 2015 (PSEL), previously the ISLLC standards. Lastly, a summary of the key points of the chapter is provided, along with a comprehensive case study, and several exercises and discussion questions.

Chapter 3 covers the instructional leadership and improvement responsibility of the position. Topics include developing a district culture of improvement, implementing instructional strategies, and developing a measurable instructional framework. A key part of the chapter includes the evaluating and implementing of instructional accountability. Several examples and sample instructional strategies are also included in this chapter along with a concluding case and discussion questions.

Chapter 4 discusses the role of the superintendent in politics and school governance. Topics include building school district capacity for governance and developing and implementing district policy. The politics of balancing the work of the school board, the district stakeholders, and the community members is discussed. A challenging and realistic case study is included at the end of the chapter to test comprehension of the material.

Chapter 5 covers the superintendent role of supervisor, evaluator, mentor, and advocate for accountability in professional growth. Standards and professional development are linked to goal setting. In addition, examples are provided of professional learning and growth plans. Like the other chapters, a concluding case and discussion questions are included.

The topic of building capacity for school district personnel and resource management is covered in chapter 6. Other areas include managing resources and personnel, and managing programs for compliance and growth. The chapter concludes with a comprehensive case study and discussion questions.

The superintendent as steward is covered in the seventh chapter. The focus is on understanding the superintendent's role in making financial decisions and recognizing the attributes of a well-managed fiscal operation. The alignment of resources to improve student outcomes is discussed as well as efficiency and effectiveness. The chapter concludes with a case study and discussion questions.

The final chapter discusses how superintendents can benchmark district oversight and performance. Benchmarks for administrative leadership, school boards, human resources, financial stability, teaching and learning, and student-centric budgeting are discussed. Analytics are discussed as a strategy to map trends, predict outcomes, and communicate with the public.

At the end of the book there are several helpful resources. Some of these include professional leadership standards and professional development growth plans, Web site resources, and references. These reference materials can be very useful in understanding district leadership, instructional improvement, and accountability.

FEATURES OF THE BOOK

This book is unique in that it provides many engaging examples that can be used by all district leaders. One feature of the book is the correlation of the objectives of each chapter with the professional leadership standards from the Educational Leadership Constituent Council (ELCC), and the former Interstate School Leaders Licensure Consortium (ISLLC), now the Professional Standards for Educational Leaders, 2015 (PSEL).

Another valuable feature of the book is the incorporation of diverse strategies on school district leadership, instructional improvement, collaboration, building capacity, and compensating and working with the district administrative team. They are provided in a straightforward and practical manner. The topics in this book are useful for any district administrator who desires to optimize fiscal, facility, and human resources. Other features of this book include:

- practical examples of school district resource management
- examples of basic school compensation structures
- strategies for leading and motivating the district administrative team
- models of leadership and instructional improvement at the district level
- a comprehensive description of strategic and succession planning processes
- examples of technology and instructional improvement at the district level
- presentation of research-based core competencies of district leaders
- strategies for building collaboration and teamwork at the district level.

Lastly, this book also contains a rich source of educational and reference materials so that school district leaders can apply the concepts for school management. Some of these materials include:

- case illustrations and figures in applying school district leadership and strategies
- examples of collaborative strategies that can improve academic performance
- examples of field-based educational issues
- actual examples of assessments and real-life case studies at the district level.

Chapter One

Many Hats, Many Masters

The Evolving Role of the Superintendent

OBJECTIVES

At the conclusion of this chapter you will be able to:

1. Understand and describe the historical role of the superintendent (ELCC 1, 2, 3, 6; PSEL 1, 2, 3).
2. Understand and describe the impact of standards, evaluation, certification, and accountability on the role of the superintendent (ELCC 2, 3; PSEL 4, 7, 8, 10).
3. Describe the school reform legislation affecting the role of the superintendent (ELCC 2, 3, 4, 5, 6; PSEL 9, 10).

HISTORY OF THE SUPERINTENDENCY

There is a story about an aging French revolutionary who remarked, while standing in the door of his salon as the mob ran toward the palace, "there go my people. I must find out where they are going so I can lead them" (Kennedy, 1960). On some days, many superintendents might feel very much like that French revolutionary.

Ask any educational professional to describe the role of school superintendents and you'll likely hear many different answers. Some might say "they run the district" or "they work with the Board of Education." If parents were asked and responded honestly, they likely would admit that they don't really know. It is fair to say, then, that many inside and outside of the public school system lack a deeper understanding of the scope and substance of the role of the superintendent in the education of their children.

1

What is in fact true is that superintendents play a very important role in the education of children. Their role as the executive leader of district operations as well as chief instructional leader can significantly affect the quality of teaching and learning in schools. The twenty-first-century superintendent faces unprecedented challenges and as the position continues to evolve, it will demand the best of America's public school leaders. The role of the public school superintendent has changed over the years and it is useful to briefly examine the evolution of the position and its role in American public education over the last two centuries.

The American public education system traces its origins back to 1647 when the Massachusetts Bay Colony mandated that every town within its jurisdiction establish a public school. Committees sprang up to run the institutions, and in the 1820s the state of Massachusetts made the committees independent of local governments, establishing the model for the autonomous school districts that exist throughout our country today.

Under the Tenth Amendment, the U.S. Constitution left authority over education in the hands of the states, which reserved to them all powers not explicitly given to the federal government. The states subsequently passed that authority on to local school boards. In 1779, Thomas Jefferson proposed a two-track educational system with different tracks, in his words, for the "laboring and the learned" (Race Forward, 2006).

While the position of a professional school superintendent is generally taken for granted in today's local education system, it was not always so. In the early days of American public education, the position of superintendent of schools, as we know it today, did not exist and the makeup of local boards varied from district to district.

Jefferson also introduced a proposal in the Virginia Assembly recommending that the citizens of each county elect three aldermen who would have general charge of the schools. The aldermen were to create an overseer for every ten school districts in the county. The duties included appointing and supervising teachers and examining pupils. These positions would become the forerunner of the modern superintendency.

Historically, the local superintendency developed simultaneously with state and county superintendencies. It was established by local initiative, not by constitution or statute, as were state and county superintendents. Some local superintendents supervised a single school district and others had responsibilities for multiple schools.

For more than a century, local boards were solely responsible for public education funding, standards, instruction, and results. At the turn of the century, 1890–1910, schools were placed under stronger control of local education governments as a result of reforms that followed disclosures of widespread municipal corruption in schools as well as in city offices. Reformers contended that board members elected by wards advanced their own parochial and special interests at the expense of the school district as a whole. Public sentiment argued that what was needed to counter this corruption was election at large or citywide, without any subdistrict electoral boundaries. A good school system was good for all they argued, not for just one part of the community.

They believed that the basic prerequisite for better school district management was the centralization of power in a chief executive to whom the selection board would delegate considerable authority. The school superintendent would be controlled, but only on board policies, by a board respectful of his professional expertise. Essentially, they aimed to "take education out of politics" (Kirst, 2010).

They argued that only under such a system would a superintendent make large-scale improvement and be held accountable. Even so, the position of superintendent remained largely one of data collection and distribution of state funds with little involvement or influence on educational matters. The evolving role of the superintendency in public education can be summarized by highlighting three phases of development that include the years 1837 to 1910, 1911 to 1944, and 1945 to the present (Townley, 2010). Figure 1.1 illustrates this development.

In the early years of this first phase, from 1837 to 1910, a superintendent's most immediate responsibility was the supervision of the instructional program. Analysis of the duties of the early superintendents reveals less responsibility for business management, school buildings, or finance. Superintendents considered themselves as scholars responsible for working with teachers, rather than as the schools' chief executive officers that we see today. However, by the end of this first period, the title of school chief executive officer began

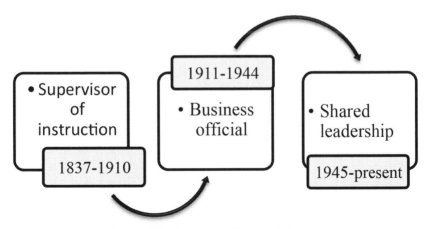

Figure 1.1. Three phases of development of the superintendency.

to appear. Responsibilities were changing to reflect the shift from a rural, ag-
riculturally based society to an increasingly urban, industrial society.

During the second phase of development, from 1911 to 1944, the superintendent assumed the responsibilities of a business official. He, or the female
who rarely occupied this position, became the executive officer of the board
of education. Business operations became the primary focus, with particular
emphasis on efficiency of operation.

During this time, universities began formal training for the superintendency
and professors of educational administration gained prominence by training
professional administrators. Columbia University, the University of Chicago,
Stanford, and Harvard were the most influential institutions in the training of
superintendents. Thousands of aspiring superintendents enrolled in these and
other universities. The view of the superintendent as businessman reached
its peak about 1930. However, as the Great Depression unfolded, the public
became disillusioned with business leadership. As a consequence, the nation
called for more democratic administrations in private as well as public organizations, including schools.

In its third phase of development, 1945 to the present, the superintendency
began to align itself with emerging management theories and shifted its focus to shared leadership. The superintendent began to share leadership with
professional organizations. State legislative bodies exerted far greater control
and influence over schools than in previous decades. This second half of the
twentieth century also saw extensive control of schools through judicial rul-
ings of state and federal courts. Control of schools by local boards also began
to diminish as unions, pressure groups, and external government agencies
usurped their traditional powers.

School boards in American public education reached their zenith in the
1930s with approximately 127,500 boards in service. Some sparsely popu-
lated states had more school board members than teachers (Griffiths, 1966).
But by the 1950s, things began to change. Figure 1.2 shows that over the next
three decades, and in particular in the 1960s, a variety of factors converged
to reduce the role of superintendents (and school boards) in the governance
of public education.

Emergence of Teachers Unions

By 1980, teachers in most areas in the United States were accelerating their
efforts to gain the right to collectively bargain for wages and benefits, resulting in the incremental decline of local school board governance. Collective
bargaining agreements between the district and teachers unions restrained
school boards and superintendents from unilaterally implementing policy.

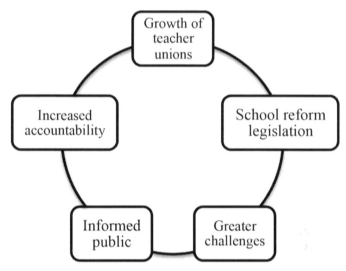

Figure 1.2. Factors affecting the role of the superintendent.

These collective bargaining agreements also restrained building-level leaders from using their own discretion on managing and leading their buildings. As a result, the role of the superintendent emerged as one of liaison between union leadership and school boards while continuing to have a less prominent role in educational issues.

Teachers organized not only to gain strong local contracts, but also to obtain preferred policies through state and national political processes. Political leaders courted them during every election cycle and political parties, especially the Democratic Party, relied on teachers unions, along with others, for political and financial support.

As teachers unions become more closely identified with other elements of the organized labor movement, their bargaining power increased. This further diminished the power of school boards and superintendents who incrementally began to pivot to educational issues where they could have more direct control such as curriculum, instruction, and assessment. Over the next twenty years, the gathering storm of growing union strength and rising accountability helped to reshape the role of the superintendent.

SCHOOL REFORM LEGISLATION

New legislation also played a significant role as school boards and superintendents evolved from largely semiautonomous entities to those facing a new era of accountability. Since the release of *A Nation At Risk* in 1983 and recent reform legislation in 2016, there has been increasing evidence that American students have consistently fallen behind the rest of the world and are becoming increasingly less competitive in the global marketplace. Over the last thirty years, five major reform initiatives profoundly affected American education and altered the politics of superintendents and school boards across the country. These legislative reforms are illustrated in figure 1.3.

The debate over testing, best teaching practices, teacher quality, accountability in schools, the role of teachers unions, and the priorities of American schools began to change beginning in 1983 when the National Commission on Excellence in Education, appointed by education secretary Terrel Bell, issued a report entitled *A Nation At Risk*. This report was the result of an

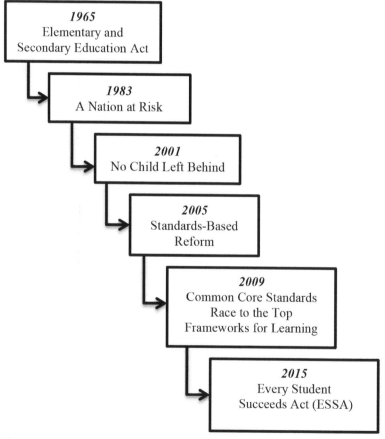

Figure 1.3.   History of modern education reform legislation.

eighteen-month study, concentrated primarily on secondary education, and found that the curriculum in American high schools as a whole no longer had a central purpose unifying all of the subjects (Brierton et al., 2015).

The report found that, in general, American education was underperforming and what was unimaginable a generation ago had begun to occur: that other nations were matching and surpassing our educational performance. One finding of this report showed that twenty-three million American adults were functionally illiterate by the simplest test of everyday reading, writing, and comprehension. The report also showed that about 13 percent of all American seventeen-year-olds could be considered functionally illiterate.

The report went on to say that the poor state of American education also could have economic repercussions. It warned that as long as American education continued to decline, our competitive edge in the global market economy would also continue to decline. The findings of this report were considered particularly depressing as the demand for highly skilled workers in both scientific and technological fields climbed to an all-time high.

As a result, the report suggested a myriad of changes and among them, five specific changes to the curriculum of American high schools. Those changes included requiring four years of English, three years of math, three years of science, three years of social studies, and half-a-year of computer science. Specific standards were established as to what should be accomplished in these five basic content areas.

The report argued that these changes would enable American students to achieve excellence as defined by the National Commission on Excellence in Education: "a school or college that sets high expectations and goals for all learners and strives in every way possible to help students reach them" (Gardner, 1983). In addition to these changes, it was also proposed that the study of foreign languages begin in the elementary schools.

As a way to increase our educational standing in the world, the commission suggested that teaching, teacher education, and education standards also be reformed. The virtues of life-long learning for all were also extolled. This report cited a high demand for increased support for those who teach mathematics, science, foreign languages, and education specialists for gifted and talented, language minority, and handicapped students.

In addition, the report found that those who were interested in the field of education were too often not academically qualified; that teacher preparation curriculum was weighted heavily with courses in education methods at the expense of courses in the subjects to be taught. The report also encouraged the raising of teacher salaries in order to attract and retain qualified teachers as well as the institution of merit pay and incentives such as grants and loans.

The impact of *A Nation At Risk* on school boards and superintendents was dramatic. For the first time since the launch of the Soviet satellite Sputnik in 1957, educators and the general public raised serious questions about the efficacy of our educational system. Those questions quickly turned to debate about teachers and classroom practice and provoked unions to go on the defensive. *A Nation At Risk* fueled a new debate between superintendents and school boards regarding student performance, teacher evaluation, and accountability. In addition, educators at every level began to revisit the validity of curriculum, instructional practice, testing, and the elements that defined a quality school.

No Child Left Behind (NCLB)

Three days after taking office in January 2001 as the forty-third President of the United States, George W. Bush announced *No Child Left Behind*, his framework for bipartisan education reform that he described as "the cornerstone of my administration." President Bush emphasized his deep belief in our public schools, but an even greater concern that "too many of our neediest children are being left behind," despite the nearly $200 billion in federal spending since the passage of the Elementary and Secondary Education Act of 1965 (ESEA).

Following the events of September 11, 2001, President Bush secured passage of the landmark *No Child Left Behind* Act of 2001 (NCLB). This new law reflected a remarkable bipartisan consensus first articulated in the President's *No Child Left Behind* framework on how to improve the performance of American elementary and secondary schools while at the same time ensuring that no child became trapped in a failing school. The law called for bipartisan solutions based on accountability, choice, and flexibility in federal education programs.

The NCLB Act, which reauthorized the Elementary and Secondary Education Act (ESEA) of 1965, incorporated the principles and strategies proposed by President Bush. These included increased accountability for states, school districts, and schools; greater choice for parents and students, particularly those attending low-performing schools; more flexibility for states and local educational agencies (LEAs) in the use of federal education dollars; and a stronger emphasis on reading, especially for our youngest children.

The key elements of the NCLB included:

- Increased accountability
- More choices for parents and students
- Greater flexibility for states, school districts, and schools
- Putting reading first

NCLB accelerated the education reform movement and caused national union leaders to become increasingly defensive regarding those reforms. Under constant criticism from several sectors, superintendents and school boards resisted union demands for improved salary and working conditions and considered new and sweeping changes in school curriculum, assessment, and instructional practice.

Standards-Based Reform

As the national education reform movement gained steam and the demand for accountability of student outcomes grew stronger, individual states moved quickly to establish their own sets of academic and curricular standards. The result of this effort was standards-based reform, a set of standards that varied widely from state to state. In addition, it become quickly apparent to school officials and teachers that these standards were not only complex and wordy in their descriptions, but also that the sheer number of standards made it impossible for teachers and schools to complete the curriculum objectives during the course of a student's educational career.

Common Core

For years it had been argued the academic progress of American students had become stagnant, and that we had lost ground to our international peers. College remediation rates remained high especially in subjects such as math. Some argued that the root cause was the uneven patchwork of academic standards that varied from state to state as well as a lack of agreement regarding what students should know and be able to do at each grade level.

As a result, it was determined that there was a need for consistent learning goals across states. In 2009, the Council of Chief State School Officers (CCSSO) and the National Governors Association (NGA) Center coordinated a state-led effort to develop the Common Core State Standards. Designed through collaboration among teachers, school chiefs, administrators, and other experts, the standards were offered as a clear and consistent framework for educators.

The Common Core claimed to be a set of high-quality academic standards in mathematics and English language arts/literacy (ELA). These learning goals outlined what a student should know and be able to do at the end of each grade. The standards were created to ensure that all students graduate from high school with the skills and knowledge necessary to succeed in college, career, and life regardless of where they live.

The Common Core also claimed to be informed by the highest, most effective standards from states across the United States and countries around the world. These standards define the knowledge and skills students should gain throughout their K–12 education in order to graduate high school and be prepared to succeed in entry-level careers, introductory academic college courses, and workforce training programs. Advocates of the Common Core Standards argue that the standards are:

- Research and evidence-based
- Clear, understandable, and consistent
- Aligned with college and career expectations
- Based on rigorous content and application of knowledge through higher-order thinking skills
- Built upon the strengths and lessons of current state standards
- Informed by other top performing countries in order to prepare all students for success in our global economy and society

The introduction of the Common Core was the next phase of the ongoing school reform movement resulting from the release of *A Nation At Risk* in 1983. For the first time in American education history, the national discussion regarding what students needed to learn and do was being driven mostly by external factors and not exclusively by superintendents and principals at the school, district, and state level. As of this writing forty-six states, the District of Columbia, four territories, and the Department of Defense Education Activity (DoDEA) have voluntarily adopted and are moving forward with the Common Core.

Race to the Top and Teacher Evaluation Reform

In 2009, president Barack Obama signed into law the American Recovery and Reinvestment Act, which among other things set aside roughly $4.35 billion for states to improve their education systems. The competition known as "Race to the Top" distributes funding to states that meet specific requirements and establish specific plans to improve their schools.

One key area of reform as laid out by the law is teacher evaluations. The discussion of teacher evaluation reform was not new and many school and union leaders agreed that most teacher evaluation systems were deeply flawed. Many in the public and private sector had argued for some time that current teacher evaluation models too often perpetuated mediocrity and even protected ineffective or unqualified teachers. What was new, however, was the discussion of linking teacher evaluations directly to student performance through a value-added model.

The idea of a value-added evaluation model and the renewed emphasis on student performance data as the most important indicator of learning sparked a whole host of reform efforts. These reform efforts subsequently led to a number of conflicts between unions, school leaders, and government officials.

The Danielson Framework for Teaching

Many states across the country have adopted the Danielson Framework for Teaching, a popular but controversial model for evaluation of teachers. Using a four-domain model, teachers are rated using specific rubrics and assigned a numerical rating. Most controversial for teachers unions is that in many districts, contracts are being renegotiated to include greater freedom to remove teachers who consistently receive poor evaluations under this model.

This reform is a direct response to the accusation by reformers that historically teachers unions have protected bad teachers and even prevented them from being fired. While the unions vigorously dispute this point, most school leaders will offer at least tacit agreement and stress that the removal of incompetent and ineffective teachers remains their most daunting challenge.

The Danielson Framework is still very new. Its true effect on the evaluation process and the extent to which it will help ensure a higher quality of teachers in our schools is yet to be seen. Many school leaders welcome this reform as a long-overdue improvement to the current evaluation process. They argue that the new model will enhance their ability to hire and retain only the best teachers for their students. As this new value-added evaluation model becomes reality in districts across the country, it will undoubtedly continue to heighten tensions between school leaders and unions.

Overall, these federal and state reform initiatives will continue to alter the political dynamic of union and administration relations. Demands from various aspects of society for greater accountability in schools will only increase pressure on teachers to raise student achievement and as a result, school leaders will suffer increasing pressure to do the same. The challenge for school leaders will be not only to implement the new model, but also to work closely with union leaders to minimize conflict and controversy as the model becomes reality.

Every Student Succeeds Act (ESSA)

The most recent education reform legislation is the Every Student Succeeds Act (ESSA) that became law in 2015. ESSA is a reauthorization of the 1965 Elementary and Secondary Education Act, which established the American federal government's expanded role in funding public education. The law replaced the unpopular No Child Left Behind Act and essentially brought school reform legislation full circle. The new law differs from NCLB in several significant ways.

There are both similarities and significant differences between ESSA and NCLB. ESSA is similar to NCLB in that states will still have to test students in reading and math in grades three through eight and once in high school. Schools are also required to break out data for the "whole school" plus different subgroups of students including English learners, students in special education, racial minorities, and those in poverty (Klein, 2016). However, states will be given wide discretion in setting goals and the protocol for holding schools and districts accountable.

States and districts will have to use locally developed, evidenced-based interventions in the bottom 5 percent of the schools where less than two-thirds of students graduate. States will also be required to flag districts where subgroup students are chronically struggling. The federal school improvement grant is gone and, in a major change departure from NCLB, the federal government will have no role in teacher evaluations.

The responsibilities of the superintendent will include a reassessment of district performance and status under NCLB, comparing the process and standing to the new ESSA law. Equally important will be the superintendent's ability to explain the new law to all staff, the Board of Education, and community stakeholders. That explanation must include a well-articulated call to action to embrace the new law as part of the overall school and district improvement plan.

The changing role of the superintendent supports the argument that the superintendent may be the single most important position in the public schools, one whose influence can extend from the curriculum to the athletic field. The superintendent's actions and leadership style can affect the climate of the school district and ultimately the very nature of the community. Because of this tremendous influence, it is imperative that superintendents reflect on the diverse needs of the community and demonstrate a high quality of servant leadership that will meet the wave of change faced by school districts across the country.

The superintendent must be an effective manager without losing touch with the instructional program and the needs of children. The effective superintendent must forcefully articulate the vision for schools and then work with widely divergent groups to bring this vision to reality. Because our communities expect schools to be sensitive to their needs and expectations, the superintendent who embraces a shared decision-making model to create community support for the schools offers the best hope for achieving transformative change.

SUMMARY

It is no surprise that the role of the superintendent has changed and evolved over more than a century-and-a-half. Schools mirror their states and local communities and, as they evolve, so will their schools and those who lead them. In the late nineteenth and first half of the twentieth centuries, the superintendent served as the manager of fiscal, physical, and personnel matters.

As the position of superintendent evolved into one of leadership in the later twentieth century, superintendents were expected, among other things, to propagate the vision and values of the school board as well as the larger school community. In their continually evolving role as leaders, they have been expected to demonstrate leadership thorough the involvement of stakeholders, the fostering of teamwork, and the building of strong relationships.

All of the above remains true today. However, as a result of a cascading series of legislative reforms over the last thirty years and increasing pressure by way of student performance data from around the world, school boards and their communities began to reexamine their own districts. What quickly followed was a call for increased academic performance by students and greater accountability for the teachers and leaders responsible for that performance.

More than just a cheerleader for good pedagogy, the modern, effective superintendent will be expected to serve as the primary instructional leader of the district, a leader of learners, prioritizing student achievement and effective instructional practices as the most important goal of the district (DiPaola & Stronge, 2003; Waters & Marzano, 2007). Moreover, the superintendent must commit the entire school district organization to a culture of continuous improvement.

CASE STUDY

You are a newly hired superintendent and have served for many years in the district as a building principal. The current superintendent has three more months in the job and, to assist you in the transition, the board of education directs you to dedicate part of your time to shadowing him. The outgoing superintendent has the reputation of being very detached from the day-to-day operation of the schools and your sense is that many staff prefer it that way. During this shadowing period, much of his advice to you reflects an "old school" attitude toward the superintendency. It appears clear to you that the outgoing superintendent's approach to the position has been more managerial and less leadership oriented, which is in sharp contrast to your own style.

What are the most important questions you will pose to the outgoing superintendent? What obstacles and challenges do you believe you might face as the new superintendent? Do you believe having been a principal in the district will be a help or a hindrance to you? What are some strategies that you might use to ease not only your own transition, but also that of your faculty, staff, and school organization in general?

EXERCISES AND DISCUSSION QUESTIONS

1. What are the most striking contrasts between the modern superintendency and the superintendents in the past? Identify three of the most striking contrasts.
2. Looking back over the evolution of the role of the superintendent, summarize the changes that have taken place and their impact on today's public education system. Identify three changes that you believe are most significant.
3. Given the challenges of twenty-first-century superintendency, what characteristics would you seek in your assistant superintendent?
4. Describe your ideal superintendent's cabinet. What personal and leadership traits would you seek as you build your team?

REFERENCES

Brierton, J., Graham, B., Tomal, D., & Wilhite, R. (2015). *Ethics and politics in school leadership*. Lanham, MD: Rowman & Littlefield. 103–109.

DiPaola, M. F., & Stronge, J. (2003). *Superintendent evaluation handbook*. Lanham, MD: Scarecrow.

Elementary and Secondary Education Amendments Act of 2011. Retrieved from https://www.govtrack.us/congress/bills/112/s1571.

Gardner, D. (1983). *A nation at risk: The imperative for educational reform. An open letter to the American people. A report to the nation and the secretary of education*. National Commission on Excellence in Education. Retrieved from http://eric.ed.gov/?id=ED226006.

Griffiths, D. E. (1966). *The school superintendent*. New York: Center for Applied Research in Education.

Kennedy, J. (1960). Remarks of senator John F. Kennedy. Rockford, IL, Coronado Theater Rally. Retrieved from http://ww.presidency.ucsb.edu/ws?pid=74197.

Kirst, M. (2010). The political and policy dynamics of K–12 education reform from 1965 to 2010: Implications for changing postsecondary education. *Research Priorities for Broad-Access Higher Education*. Center for Education Policy Analysis. Stanford University.

Klein, A. (2016, October 14). Politics K–12: NEA wants states to go for bold changes under ESSA, listen to teachers. (Web log comment). *Education Week*. Retrieved from http://blogs.edweek.org/edweek/campaign-k-12/.

Race Forward. (2006). Historical timeline of public education in the US. The Center for Racial Justice Innovation (formerly Applied Research Center). Retrieved from http://raceforward.org/research/re[orts/historical-timeline-public-education-us.

Townley, A. (2010). *The school superintendent: History of the superintendency.* Retrieved from http://www.stanswartz.com/adminbook/chap7.htm.

Waters, J. T., & Marzano, R. J. (2007, March). The primacy of superintendent leadership. *School Administrator, 64*(3), 10–16.

Chapter Two

Leading with Mastery

Core Competencies for Superintendents

OBJECTIVES

At the conclusion of this chapter you will be able to:

1. Understand school leader core competencies for the superintendents and principals (ELCC 2, 3; PSEL 1, 2, 3, 4, 9, 10).
2. Understand school leader core competencies as aligned with the ELCC and PSEL standards (ELCC 1, 2, 3, 4, 5, 6; PSEL 1, 2, 3, 4, 5, 6, 7, 8, 9, 10).
3. Understand knowledge and skill delivery systems for diverse learners (ELCC 1, 2, 4, 6; PSEL 3, 4, 5).
4. Understand strategies for development and implementation of the professional learning community model (ELCC 1, 2, 6; PSEL 4, 6, 7).

SUPERINTENDENT CORE COMPETENCIES

In order to effectively lead school districts, superintendents must demonstrate twelve core competencies. By definition, competencies differ from traits. A trait is a characteristic, a feature, an attribute. A competency is the ability to do something successfully. It is skill, a talent, a level of mastery. It is less about who superintendents are and more about what they can successfully accomplish.

The concept of leadership traits has been well covered in the literature of educational leadership. The challenges faced by the modern school superintendent demand more than just traits. Today, effective school leader traits are expected to be present in those who seek the role of leadership. Those aspiring to be school superintendents would be well advised to recognize that the measure of the twenty-first-century school superintendent will be in what they can accomplish, what they can do.

While a few of these competencies may be exclusive to the work of the school superintendent, most cut across the broad spectrum of competencies inherent to any executive leadership role. More directly said, all twelve competencies apply to leading any organization, but some are especially important in leading school organizations. Figure 2.1 illustrates the twelve core superintendent competencies. These competencies are interrelated but, under closer examination, also present inherent challenges for the superintendent. Both competencies and challenges will be explored in this chapter.

Core Competency #1: School Governance (Collaborating with School District Board Members in Policy Development)

Effective school superintendents have always had to be highly competent in managing schools and leading school boards to craft policy and govern the district. This will undoubtedly remain a high priority of all superintendents and school boards. For many, a source of confusion for many is an understanding of who actually "runs" the district. Is it the school board or the

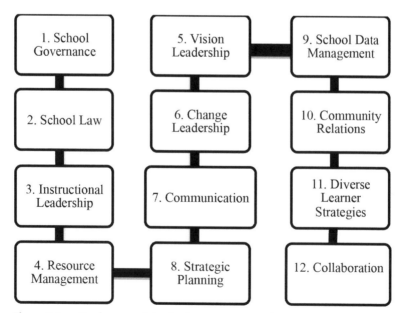

Figure 2.1.   Twelve superintendent core competencies.

superintendent? The answer is simple. While superintendents are responsible for many aspects of the operation of the district, they report to and serve at the pleasure of the board of education. The superintendent is, then, the agent of the board of education.

Superintendents and their cabinets or administrative teams often propose new policies or a change to existing policies. These policies and changes may by driven by changes in the law, the emergence of a problem or situation that warrants administrative action, or pressure from community or stakeholder groups. For example, a new law may require policy or procedural changes regarding student physicals or a change in the graduation requirements. Parents may lobby for a change in the start time for the school day or the process for admission to student activities or athletics. Unions may lobby the board for noncontractual policies that affect their members.

The effective superintendent must be able to successfully collaborate with the school board to move the district forward. The board is typically comprised of seven unique personalities who rarely agree, with any unanimity, on anything. They may have run for the school board for many reasons including a bona fide desire to improve the district, a personal agenda for a particular policy change, or a specific axe to grind with the district, teachers, the union, or even the superintendent. This unique blend of personalities shapes the core of the challenge for the superintendent.

With the right board, a dynamic, visionary superintendent can have a profound influence on the scope of change to the district. This would, however, require a board that trusts their superintendent and allows him or her considerable latitude in making decisions. A board of education that is highly politicized, very strong-willed, or simply predisposed to assert its own authority will likely attempt to obstruct the superintendent who attempts to demonstrate strong, assertive leadership, especially when the superintendent attempts to change or affect the existing status quo.

The challenge this competency presents is rooted in the superintendent's ability to cultivate relationships with the board of education and the community it represents. The relationship between the superintendent, the board of education, and the community it represents is, by nature, political. To some extent, the superintendent has always played the role of politician. But in this new era of high-stakes accountability, the political skills of the superintendent will most certainly be tested.

Politics is said to be the "art of the possible," and so it is critical that the superintendent, especially a new superintendent, builds and cultivates relationships with each individual board member so that conflict and politics within the board can be eliminated or at least tempered. By extension, the same is true for key members of the community including parents. Failure to seize every opportunity to galvanize the community to the mission of the district may result in conflict or gridlock in policy development, organizational change, and school improvement.

Savvy superintendents also understand that to engage only the community leaders and ignore the parents, the taxpayers who pay their way, is a recipe for early failure. When a crisis comes, and it will come, the political capital resulting from relationships with the board of education and members of the community can provide welcome support. Without it, oppositional forces in the district or the community who want the superintendent to fail will quickly organize and show themselves.

The other challenge faced by superintendents as they seek to enhance this competency is the need to lead a collaborative governance process with the board. Superintendents are the architects not just of the district and its path forward, but also of the relationship between seven board members and a multitude of stakeholders within the school district. Effective and resilient superintendents understand that as servant leaders, they serve many masters within the greater school community. Those masters include the board of education, teachers and staff, students, and the ever-important community of parents and taxpayers.

Core Competency #2: School Law (Understanding Legal Issues Impacting District Policy and Operations)

One of the most intimidating dilemmas of school leadership, and certainly for the superintendent, is the need to follow the law closely while recognizing their own inadequacy regarding the intricacies of those same laws. Unless the superintendent has a law degree, which is rare, they will frequently consult with the attorney who represents the school district when in doubt as to how to proceed. When asked how they ensure the law is being followed, some superintendents have been known to remark, "I keep our attorney on speed dial."

Regardless of access to attorney advice, a core competency for any superintendent is a broad but working knowledge of the legal issues that may impact district policies and operations. This may include laws that impact employment, human resource policies such as hiring, firing, and disciplinary action for students and staff, along with inevitable rounds of collective bargaining negotiations. Special education brings its own byzantine collection of legal issues that can change from year to year. Health and welfare issues regarding immunization requirements, medical and personal records for students and staff, and, of course, the need to ensure confidentiality of both must be considered within the context of the law.

Superintendents are also stewards of the financial resources of the district so it is important that they understand the law regarding the use of taxpayer money. As one might expect, there are also a myriad of other issues that arise in the course of the school year and these typically are managed on a situational basis. That's why many superintendents will note that their education regarding school law increases exponentially with every school year.

The inherent challenge embedded in this core competency is less about direct knowledge of the law and more about ensuring that the laws are followed across the school organization. While it is important for the effective superintendent to have a working knowledge of school law, it is even more important that the superintendent builds a culture where all personnel understand and respect the need to observe those laws and takes measures to ensure that laws are being followed.

More than one superintendent has been removed because someone in the district, without his or her knowledge, breaks a law. Unfortunately, "I didn't know" is not a defense in a court of law, in the eyes of the board of education, or in the court of public opinion. Every aspect of the district is, first and foremost, the responsibility of the superintendent. The superintendent's leadership team must also understand their responsibilities regarding the law. That is why effective superintendents hire the best and the brightest district- and building-level leaders to ensure that laws governing district policies and operations are consistently followed.

Core Competency #3: Instructional Leadership (Demonstrating Proactive, Engaged Leadership for District Improvement of Instruction)

The role of the modern superintendent has evolved considerably over the last several decades. Once relegated to largely policy implementation and data gathering, the twenty-first-century superintendent faces a plethora of new and ever-changing K–12 standards as well as increased accountability and global comparison. The leadership of curriculum, instruction, and assessment issues is now included in the duties of superintendents, casting them in new roles as instructional leaders. Effective superintendents are wise to recognize that student achievement data will now dominate their professional conversations and can have profound effects on their schools and district.

Duties that once were the exclusive responsibility of curriculum professionals within a district are now being shifted across school organizations. Organizational charts are being flattened as professional learning communities comprised of small teams of teachers collaborate to determine skill-driven curriculums, effective instructional practices, and valid and reliable assessments. Decisions are being driven down to the smallest team.

It is important to note that even the most effective superintendent cannot be an expert in curriculum, instruction, and assessment for all subjects

and all grade levels. In a shared leadership model, subordinate professionals will lead in these areas. But the effective superintendent recognizes the
importance of being proactive, involved, and engaged. Most of all, superintendents must ensure that effective knowledge delivery systems are being
consistently used across the school organization. Figure 2.2 illustrates the
integrated nature of the components of the district model for knowledge and
skill delivery systems.

To do that, they must know how to identify modern and relevant curriculums, best instructional practices, the most authentic assessments, and
the technology systems necessary to support these three important elements.
The superintendent's foundational knowledge of all four components will be
greatly enhanced by conversing, collaborating, and engaging with those professionals directly involved in that knowledge delivery system.

The effective superintendent recognizes that instruction leadership demands the propagation of four critical questions that must drive academic
decisions across the school organization.

1. What do we want . . . our students to know and be able to do?
2. How do we know . . . our students know it and can do it?
3. What do we do when . . . our students don't know it and can't do it?
4. What do we do when . . . our students already know it and can already
   do it?

Figure 2.2.   Knowledge and skill delivery system.

Core Competency #4: Resource Management (Managing Financial, Facility, and Human Resources Processes and Regulations)

The superintendent is the steward of taxpayer dollars which in turn provide the resources necessary to operate the district. Superintendents have a fiduciary responsibility to manage these resources in an ethical and responsible manner. This includes financial resources such as state aid, grants, tuition payments, academic and athletic fees, activity fees, and any other money that flows through the district. While the superintendent may rely on an assistant superintendent for business, or a business manager, the ultimate responsibility for the proper use of financial resources rests with the superintendent.

It is fair to say that most superintendents who find themselves in trouble do so because of the misuse of financial resources. This trouble typically results from improper commingling of money, use of district finances for personal use, improper use of grant money, or failure to accurately and honestly report to the state the manner in which financial resources are being used. Regardless of who has the direct responsibility for financial management, the superintendent, as the chief executive, would be wise to trust but verify.

The superintendent also bears the ultimate responsibility for the stewardship and management of the district facilities. Depending on the size of the district, this can consume much of the superintendent's time especially if a major construction project, such as an addition or remodeling, is undertaken. The effective superintendent knows that it is critically important to hire only the best building and grounds leaders and personnel so that facilities are managed effectively and in a proactive manner.

Nothing will erode the morale and attitude of staff, as well as the overall climate of the school organization, faster than poorly managed facilities. Savvy superintendents know that there is little hope of the staff embracing their vision for the district when buildings are too cold or too hot, grounds are poorly maintained, and classrooms lack technology and equipment to effectively deliver instruction.

With that said, technology presents a unique challenge to the twenty-first-century superintendent. With technology changing at an ever-increasing rate, effective superintendents must hire the most competent, innovative technology experts to manage technology while at the same time becoming competent themselves in key aspects of education technology.

Savvy superintendents know that more and newer technology is not, in itself, a solution that will solve every problem and raise the achievement levels of all students. But they also know that without a realistic, sustainable, multiyear technology plan, they can never hope to offer their students and teachers the world-class learning environment they deserve. Without that environment, students will continue to fall behind other students at home and around the world.

Superintendents must also manage their most important resource, human resources. In his landmark book, *Good to Great*, author Jim Collins advised leaders to consider "first who, then what" (Collins, 2001). Effective leaders of world-class organizations know that their people are their most valuable resource. If the mission and vision of the organization has any hope of being accomplished, that organization must employ the best professionals available, treat them with respect and kindness, and hold them accountable for performance. The first two are easy. The third one is much more difficult.

A fast track to corrupting the performance of a school organization is to allow underperformers to continue to do so. If this occurs, before long the top performers will either leave or begin to underperform themselves. New York mayor Rudy Giuliani is said to have displayed a sign on his desk, "everyone is accountable all of the time" (Giuliani, 2002). It must be pointed out, though, that effective superintendents as leaders don't lead by fear. They lead by striking an artful balance between treating their faculty and staff with respect, kindness, and professionalism while clearly communicating the expectation that as professionals, they will be expected to perform at the highest level. Transformational superintendents are multipliers of the talent in their organizations. They make all their people better.

This core competency presents a unique challenge due to the scope of the responsibility of managing all the resources of the district. For example, it is easy for a superintendent to become consumed with facilities management because it's immediate and tangible. Human resources issues can be all consuming as well. Issues involving union grievances, employee discipline, and hiring and dismissals are never-ending. The ability to manage the broad scope of all the resources in the district will challenge even the best superintendents.

Financial issues can also weigh heavily as they include funding challenges, budget shortfalls, and even Freedom of Information Act (FOIA) requests. Again, the effective superintendent usually has people to manage these issues but few of them will act unilaterally without asking the counsel of the superintendent. The day often can be filled with cabinet members standing in your doorway, saying, "we have a problem" or "do you have a minute?"

So, if effective superintendents seek to resolve the issue of time management, what will be their focus? Knowing that the "buck" stops with them, how much decision-making latitude are they willing to give their team as they attempt to manage the myriad of resources that are so critical to district operation? What is their level of trust and what mechanisms are in place so that they can trust, but verify?

Core Competency #5: Vision Leadership (Leading and Motivating Staff to Achieve School and District Improvement Goals)

Of all the competencies, the need to lead and motivate staff, or what some have called the "vision thing," presents the greatest challenge and, some might argue, is in short supply among too many of today's superintendents. Vision might be the most difficult competency to explain to the aspiring superintendent. One might begin by saying that the superintendent, as manager, sees only what is, what currently exists. The superintendent, as a true leader, sees the district as it might be. Or, as Robert Kennedy said, "Some people see things as they are and ask why, I see things that never were and ask why not" (Kennedy, 1968).

Visionary superintendents have the ability to imagine what those in the district can accomplish together. They have the ability to craft a vision with their stakeholders and then articulate and declare that vision proudly and publicly. They provide a compass for school improvement, ensuring that everyone in the organization remains focused on the vision. They are the cheerleader for the vision and the one who lifts the organization when failures, and there will be failures, occur. Most importantly, they inspire. They inspire others with the vision. Simon Sinek, author of *Leaders Eat Last*, notes that in his famous speech in 1963 Dr. Martin Luther King, Jr. did not say, "I have a plan." He said, "I have a dream" (Sinek, 2014). Truly effective superintendents recognize that vision drives the plan, not the other way around. School improvement begins with vision and a compelling imagination of what the district might ultimately become.

The challenge of this competency is not that superintendents lack vision. Some may but, generally, it is reasonable to say that most superintendents come to their positions with a vision for the district. The board of education, if they are doing their due diligence, will certainly want to hear about that vision before hiring a superintendent. So what causes it not to be realized?

The critical question is whether they can inspire others to that vision. Are they able to clearly articulate the path to accomplishing the vision? Do they have the skills to galvanize the faculty and staff to a common cause? If they cannot, there is little hope of accomplishing anything of significance. They might become reasonably effective managers of the status quo, but they likely will never move the district from good to great.

Core Competency #6: Change Leadership (Leading and Managing School and District Change Initiatives)

Closely related to vision is the core competency of change leadership. It is unlikely that new superintendents will be asked to maintain the status quo.

If they are following a failed or underperforming superintendent, they will be asked to repair the damage done and move the district forward. If they follow a successful superintendent, they will be asked to continue the work and advance the improvement of the district. Either way, change and leading change will be embedded in the work of the superintendent. More than merely introducing change, the superintendent must be able to lead and sustain the conversation about change and convince stakeholders that change is in the best interests of the district and the community.

Effective superintendents will need to understand the nature of change and its likely effect on the entire school community. Many well-intentioned superintendents who have failed after attempting to disrupt a long-standing status quo lament that they did not anticipate the visceral, negative reaction of faculty, staff, and, in particular, their unions. By understanding the impact of change on the organization, effective superintendents tap into the school organization's capacity not only for change, but also for the rate of change. They can anticipate the organizational angst as change occurs. Savvy superintendents understand that old political axiom that perception is reality and that optics matter.

The manner in which change is rolled out is also directly linked to its success. Moving too quickly can have disastrous results while moving too slowly can result in a loss of interest and a lessening of positive outcome. Some will complain that the system moves too slowly and argue for a faster rate of change. Some will argue to "make haste slowly" and take the time to get it right. Effective superintendents understand the need to balance both; to maintain a sense of urgency and a bias for action; to use prudent judgment tempered by collaboration with those affected by change including parents, teachers, students, union leadership, and community leaders. The successful superintendent also recognizes that perfect can be the enemy of good and that, subsequently, good can be the enemy of great.

Core Competency #7: Communication (Communicating to School District Faculty, Staff, and Stakeholders)

Communication has always been a core competency for school leaders, including superintendents as well as leaders of any organization. Examine any book on leadership in the last twenty years and it will surely include many pages on the importance of communication. The effective superintendent recognizes that communication has evolved much like the job itself. Once upon a time, the superintendent communicated by way of staff meetings, memorandums, and newsletters. Today, the explosion of social media, including Facebook, Twitter, automated voice and email messaging, Web sites, and smartphone technology has opened up a myriad of new opportunities to communicate across a wider spectrum of stakeholders than ever before.

The savvy superintendent also knows that these same technological tools can be a blessing and a curse. Information travels farther and faster than ever before. This may inhibit the superintendent from making prudent, well-thought-out decisions before the people affected by the decision are demanding answers. The need to manage a crisis before it shows up on Facebook or Twitter challenges the superintendent to embed new protocols into the culture of the school organization. Doing so will challenge even the most experienced leaders. Information shared on social media may travel well beyond its desired location. The overuse of automated calls and emails to parents can quickly numb them to their importance and cause them to be ignored much like traditional print messages or letters sent home.

Today's effective superintendents recognize that they are leading an organization brimming with not only students, but also younger, millennial staff who are digital natives and expect to receive communication via modern platforms. They must also understand that these tools of communication can be both an asset and a liability depending how they are managed. But, no matter how modern the communication tool, effective superintendents are expected to clearly articulate information and their vision, and to inspire their organization to follow. Those who cannot, or will not, are best to heed the advice of Benjamin Disraeli, the once-great prime minister of the United Kingdom, who reminded all leaders that, "With words, we govern men" (Reiniers, 2012).

Core Competency #8: Strategic Planning (Developing and Establishing School District Performance Goals)

Today, a core competency and responsibility of a superintendent is to lead the process of strategic planning for the district. The board of education will look to the superintendent to educate, guide, and lead them and the community in this very important process. The process will require the gathering of needs assessment data from all stakeholders, convening a strategic planning committee comprised of a representation of those stakeholders, and then bringing them all together to build the plan.

The strategic plan will serve as the overarching vision statement for the district. Once formed, the strategic planning committee will be tasked with setting goals and a process to achieve them. The completed and board-approved strategic plan will likely span three to five years and if vibrant, will serve as a living document and a touchstone for the entire school community as the work of school improvement moves forward.

Core Competency #9: School Data Management
(Interpreting and Using Assessment and Other School Data)

In today's high-stakes testing environment, with so much public scrutiny on both district academic and financial data, the effective superintendent will need a thorough understanding of how data are gathered, interpreted, and used. Data-driven decision-making now anchors most strategic planning in school districts across the country. Data must be gathered effectively but more importantly, they must be easily analyzed and accessible to school professionals to assist them in adjusting curriculum, instruction, and assessment strategies. Districts that fail to do so will quickly find themselves drowning in data with no ability to leverage those data for change and improvement.

Today, it would be difficult to find an educational leader who disputes the value of using accurate data in the decision-making process. School professionals across the country are using empirical data to make decisions about curriculum, instruction, assessment, and evaluation. The challenge for the effective superintendent will be to recognize the need to embed the use of data in the district culture while at the same time ensuring the thoughtful and reflective use of less empirical metrics, sometimes called evidence, to measure success and outcomes. Such evidence might include experience, intuition, judgment, collaboration, observational information, and the more artful aspects of teaching.

Any superintendent who worships at the altar of data while failing to recognize the value of other evidence will likely experience an erosion of confidence and trust among the very professionals who are tasked with acting on those data. Savvy superintendents know that human intelligence, not numbers alone, is a vital component of measuring the high-performing school organization. They also know that relentless reliance on data can demoralize the professionals who serve children and parents. The effective superintendent must be able to balance the use of both.

Core Competency #10: Community Relations (Developing Positive Relationships and Partnerships with Community Members)

Once upon a time, a primary responsibility and a board-of-education expectation of superintendents was their interaction and relationship-building with the community. While that role still certainly exists, the emerging role of the superintendent as instructional leader has altered that dynamic somewhat. In addition to a long list of responsibilities, the superintendent is expected to be the chief instructional leader for the district. Ensuring a high quality of teaching and learning, once largely the responsibility of principals, has now been added to the superintendent's job description. New and better technology communication tools also have expanded and enhanced the relationship between the superintendent and the community.

The greatest community relations challenge for the effective, twenty-first-century superintendent is to leverage the power of community involvement to enhance school district improvement and support. In a very real sense, today's superintendent is now the chief public relations officer for the district. With financial resources dwindling, the superintendent must educate the community on the cost of a world-class education and what such an education will do for the future of their children.

In order to meet this challenge, effective superintendents must possess a deep understanding of their communities, their values, aspirations, and expectations. The use of discussion forums, parent advisory committees, town hall meetings, and social media platforms can make connections and build bridges that will coalesce the community and create authentic partnerships between the community and the district. Meeting this challenge will demand a special kind of leader who understands the positive optics of being visible in the community; one who truly enjoys engaging the public and recognizes that the benefits of such a relationship for the district are without limits.

Competency #11: Diverse Learner Strategies (Ensuring Effective Instruction for Diverse Learners)

As the chief instructional leader for the school district, the effective superintendent must ensure that the needs of all learners are being consistently and effectively served. In addition to the mainstream group of learners, superintendents and their boards of education face a growing challenge to meet the needs of additional groups of diverse learners who require specialized services. These groups are illustrated in figure 2.3. This includes special education students, gifted students, English learners (EL), and early childhood learners. Embedded in these four major diverse learner groups shown are also groups known as subsets that include minority students, students in poverty, students with social-emotional struggles, and students who consistently struggle for a variety of reasons.

The four groups of diverse learners and their subsets all require awareness, advocacy, and creative solutions to ensure that they are fully included in the broader learning community. Superintendents, as leaders of the whole district, must have both an acute awareness as well as a deep understanding of the needs of these diverse learning groups. They must become the champion of all students by ensuring that curriculum, instruction, and assessments incorporate strategies that fully recognize and meet the needs of diverse learners.

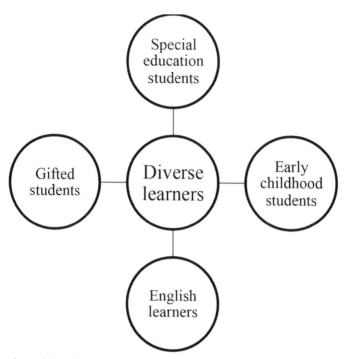

Figure 2.3. Diverse learner groups.

The effective superintendent, as a true servant leader, must be fully prepared to represent these and any other student groups in the school that may have been historically underserved. Doing so will test the ability of the superintendent to balance the resources of the district to also ensure equity for all students. Striking an equitable balance in a world of shrinking resources will require a very special leader.

Competency #12: Collaboration (Building a Collaborative Culture across the School Organization)

Of all the superintendent competencies, none is more important than the ability to foster collaboration across the district. The concept of professional learning communities, when effectively implemented, has transformed many school districts into learning organizations where professionals gather together to analyze and act on data and evidence. The superintendent must be able to clearly articulate what it means to be a professional learning community. They must clarify what it means to be a learning organization and define collaboration as "co-labor" where professionals share effective practices and are mutually accountable to each other for positive outcomes for students.

The effective superintendent recognizes that consensus will not be achieved by mere declaration; it is not enough to simply announce that the district will be a professional learning community where collaboration will be the key. Consensus must be actively and consistently fashioned over time. Dr. Martin Luther King Jr. once remarked that "a genuine leader is not a seeker of consensus but a molder of consensus" (King, 1967).

Richard DuFour, noted author on the topic of professional learning communities, explains the professional learning community phenomenon this way: "The professional learning community model flows from the assumption that the core mission of formal education is not simply to ensure that students are taught but to ensure that they learn. This simple shift—from a focus on teaching to a focus on learning—has profound implications for schools" (DuFour et al., 2010).

Use of common language to describe the professional learning community is important, especially when it comes to understanding the integration of the professional learning community model across the district. Effective superintendents understand and can clearly articulate this model to all sections of the school organization as well as its stakeholders. As the model in figure 2.4 shows, the district as a whole makes up the greater professional learning community. The building is comprised of smaller learning communities

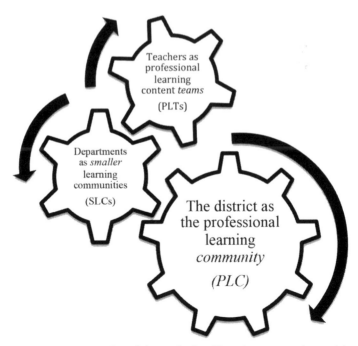

Figure 2.4. Integration of the professional learning community model.

comprised of grade levels, or departments or divisions. More deeply embedded are small teams of teachers acting as professional learning teams who are laser-focused on curriculum content, instructional delivery, and assessment development and analysis of the data they generate.

The effective superintendent knows that this model reflects a true professional learning community. It is a process, not a program, and defines the interrelational nature of the professional work of educators. As the professional learning community collaborative culture evolves over time, much of the decision-making is driven down to a small team of professionals. Within the larger community the superintendent utilizes smaller teams of teachers—professional learning teams—to gather, analyze, and act on the data. Building-level school leaders, also acting as their own collaborative team, guide the professional learning teams and ensure accountability for collaboration and outcome.

The professional learning community/professional learning team model takes time to develop. However, the most effective superintendents foster a district culture where professionals possess a sense of urgency, a bias for action—one where they recognize that every professional is accountable, and accountable to each other first; that each member of the team has a responsibility to honor their commitment to each other and, by extension, to all of their students.

Effective superintendents must ensure that there is a deep and common understanding of the collaborative model across the district; that there must be a shared commitment to creating a learning school as opposed to a teaching school. A learning school is focused and serves the needs of students. A teaching school focuses, either accidentally or deliberately, on the needs of the adults in the organization. Superintendents must drive out the fear in the organization so that faculty and staff are empowered to speak truth to power, are not afraid to innovate, and are comfortable engaging each other honestly and with candor.

The core challenge for the superintendent, then, is to foster a culture where everyone in the district recognizes a common accountability for collaboration. Effective superintendents foster a collaborative culture where all the professionals in the district recognize that the era of the independent educator is over and that twenty-first-century schools in our "new, flat world" must become laboratories of shared commitment, true collaboration, and bold innovation.

SUMMARY

The role of the school superintendent has evolved significantly over the last century. What was once a supervisory position has now become a job for a level-five leader (Collins, 2001). The twenty-first-century superintendent faces unprecedented challenges that include not just high-stakes testing and accountability but a rapidly changing demographic, especially in our urban centers, new and constantly evolving technologies, problems linked to the continued disruption of the nuclear family, an increasingly dissatisfied and impatient public, and, more than ever before, global comparison and competition in a "new, flat world."

Not only will our graduates be competing in the global marketplace against graduates from around the world, but the constituencies that fund our school districts will also continue to compare our schools to those around the world. The effective superintendent must possess all the competencies discussed in this chapter. They will come to their positions with different levels of skill in each area. Every superintendent must commit to developing each competency to its fullest.

All will face unique challenges in the context of different districts. Changing an arthritic school system resistant to change and stalled by continued allegiance to the status quo and what Steve Case (2016) calls "legacy dogma" will not be easy. It will require hard work, courage, and relentless perseverance, and it will not be for the faint of heart.

Embedded in all twelve competencies is the need for superintendents to exhibit a sense of urgency, a bias for action, a vision for the future of the district, and the ability to inspire, challenge, and motivate educational professionals to challenge the status quo and reboot professionals' passion for leading students, teachers, and schools to success. In the opening pages of his book, *Leaders Eat Last*, Simon Sinek (2014) offers a clarion call to all who aspire to be leaders, including those who seek to lead as superintendents of schools:

Leaders are the ones who run headfirst into the unknown.
They rush toward the danger.
They put their own interests aside to protect us or to pull us into the future.
Leaders would sooner sacrifice what is theirs to save what is ours.
And they would never sacrifice what is ours to save what is theirs.
This is what it means to be a leader.
It means they choose to go first into danger, headfirst toward the unknown.
And when we feel sure they will keep us safe,
We will march behind them and work tirelessly to see their visions come to life,
And proudly call ourselves their followers (Sinek, 2014).

CASE STUDY

You are the superintendent of a large suburban high school district. The district is mostly white with a small African American population. Recently, in one of your high schools, a white male student made several racial slurs toward several African American girls. The parents of the girls are demanding expulsion for the male student and have mobilized high-profile civil rights activists and the local news to underscore their demands.

The parents of the white, male student are insisting that expulsion is unfair and violates the district's disciplinary guidelines for due process. The controversy is spreading to your other schools and tensions are rising between student groups. The board of education is insisting that you resolve this issue soon and as low profile as possible. How will you facilitate a resolution to this conflict? What will be your first step? Consider all the competencies discussed in this chapter as you consider your options.

EXERCISES AND DISCUSSION QUESTIONS

1. You are a new superintendent in a small elementary district. Describe your strategy for introducing a collaborative, professional learning community model to the district. What will be your first steps? What challenges or obstacles do you anticipate and do you have a strategy for overcoming them?
2. In a recent election, three of the board members who hired you as superintendent were not reelected. You have become aware that one of them does not approve of your leadership style. Another of the new members is the parent of a gifted student in the district and you suspect she has a personal agenda for being on the board. The last, new member is an unknown. Describe your strategy for establishing and cultivating a positive relationship with the three new members.
3. The board of education has asked you to organize and lead the effort to craft a three-year strategic plan. The first decision you must make is whether to lead the process yourself as superintendent or to hire a consultant to facilitate the process. What factors will affect your decision? Once that decision is made, what are your next steps? What will be the key features of your communication plan as the plan is developed?
4. You are a newly appointed superintendent promoted to the position after five years in the district as a principal. Initially, the school board was very supportive of your appointment but soon after you started, it seemed that they would prefer that you not become involved in policymaking and confine yourself to largely public relations and general district management tasks. How will you go about establishing yourself as the new superintendent? What strategies will you use to convince the board that you need to

be closely involved with the board in crafting policy? What obstacles do you anticipate and what is your plan for overcoming those obstacles?

5. As the superintendent and "chief instructional leader" of a large elementary district, what is your plan for involving yourself in curriculum, instructional, and assessment issues? How will you do so and take measures so that you don't overstep and interfere with the role of your principals? What will be your top priority in your first year as superintendent as it pertains to instructional leadership?

6. Discuss superintendent competency #1. How do you balance your responsibility to the board you serve and still remain courageous enough to advocate for what you believe is best for teaching and learning, for teachers and students? What are your core values, your nonnegotiables? Is there anything worth fighting for or is everything open to compromise and capitulation? Be specific.

REFERENCES

Case, S. (2016). *The third wave: An entrepreneur's vision of the future.* New York: Simon & Schuster.

Collins, J. (2001). *Good to great: Why some companies make the leap . . . and others don't.* New York: HarperCollins.

DiPaola, M. F., & Stronge, J. (2003). *Superintendent evaluation handbook.* Lanham, MD: Scarecrow.

DuFour, R., DuFour, R., Eaker, R., & Many, T. (2010). *Learning by doing: A handbook for professional communities at work. A practical guide for PLC and leadership teams.* Bloomington, IN: Solution Tree Press.

Giuliani, R. (2002). *Leadership.* New York: Miramax Books.

Kennedy, R. (1968). Remarks at the University of Kansas. Retrieved from http://images2.americanprogress.org/campus/email/RobertFKennedyUniversityofKansas.pdf.

King, M. L., Jr. (1967). Domestic impact of the war. Speech to the National Labor Leadership Assembly for Peace. *African-American involvement in the Vietnam War: Speeches and sounds.* Retrieved from http://www.aavw.org/special_features/speeches_speech_king03.html.

Reiniers, J. (2012, September 12). With words we govern men. *Hernando Today.* Retrieved from http://hernandotoday.com/with-words-we-govern-men/.

Sinek, S. (2014). *Leaders eat last. Why some teams pull together and others don't.* New York: Penguin Group.

Chapter Three

Leading with Intent: A Third Way

The Superintendent as Learning Leader

OBJECTIVES

At the conclusion of this chapter you will be able to:

1. Apply the school leader core competencies in developing a district culture of improvement (ELCC 2, 3; PSEL 4, 6, 7, 10).
2. Apply the superintendent core competencies in implementing effective instructional strategies for improved student learning (ELCC 2, 3; PSEL 4, 5, 6, 7).
3. Apply the school leader core competencies for integrating instructional leadership and school district improvement (ELCC 2, 3, 4; PSEL 4, 5, 6, 7, 10).
4. Describe the role of the superintendent in developing a district culture for positive learning and growth (ELCC 2, 3, 4; PSEL 6, 7, 8, 10).

THE ROLE AND FUNCTION OF THE SUPERINTENDENT

In many ways, the job of the superintendent is similar to any chief executive officer in any other organization. As executive leaders, they work with budgets, facilities, management, contracts, evaluations, community relations, disgruntled constituents, and they attend endless meetings. But what are the unique roles and core competencies of school superintendents? How do these roles and core competencies differ from school principals? And, how do these roles and core competencies support the improvement of the organizational culture and overall performance of the school district? How do they come to serve as chief learning leaders?

Like most everything else in education today, the role of leaders is changing and evolving. This should come as no surprise to anyone in public education. After all, we need only to look back on the more recent history of public education to see that it has always been the responsibility of the leader to implement the cascading series of legislative reforms resulting from the publication of *A Nation At Risk* in 1983. Throughout the history of American public education, the role of the superintendent has also evolved as part of the shifting landscape of educational reform. Again, this should come as no surprise. What might come as a surprise, however, is the more recent paradigm shift surrounding the role of the superintendent.

The traditional role of the superintendent is well defined in the educational literature. Spanning several decades, the role of the superintendent has been discussed in the context of teacher-scholar, manager, democratic leader, applied social scientist, and communicator (Kowalski, 2005). More specifically, it has been described as a steward of the district's financial resources, and a manager of district operations, facilities, and personnel. The superintendent is also seen as the leader of the mission and vision of the district, and certainly as the liaison between the district and the elected school board. An examination of the history of the superintendency will likely reveal some variation on a combination of these themes.

One description of the superintendent's role, that of "loose coupling," is useful because it draws a compelling contrast to the current role of learning leader. Since its emergence in the 1960s, the idea of loose coupling described the elusive and largely unsuccessful quest over the past century for school administrators who can serve as "instructional leaders." Most credentialing programs for superintendents and principals claim to prepare the next generation of instructional leaders, and professional development for educational leaders at least alleges to have instructional leadership as its focus (Gehrman, 2008, citing Elmore, 2004).

An honest appraisal of the work of superintendents and other educational leaders points to a different pattern however; that direct involvement in instruction is among the least frequent activities performed by administrators of any kind at any level, and those who do engage in instructional leadership activities on a consistent basis are a relatively small proportion of the total school administrative force (Cuban, 1988; Murphy, 1990).

The question then becomes: how did we get here? What is so different today? What are the internal and external forces that are profoundly changing the role of the modern superintendent? One study argues that the two most significant developments are an evolving series of reform initiatives and the resulting, and increasing, demand for greater accountability. The study goes on to say that while superintendents are interested in curriculum and instruction and believe they are important tasks, the daily realities of their work often subvert even the most committed professional (Bredeson & Kose, 2007).

It is important to recognize that a significant change in the role of the superintendent involves the scope of responsibility and, more importantly, the expectation on the part of a host of stakeholders, including boards of education, for more direct involvement with teaching and learning. The twenty-first-century superintendent is expected to be the chief educational officer, the primary leader of learning. An even more significant change, however, is the expectation that the superintendent will be directly responsible for fostering a culture of collaborative inquiry and the architect of a true learning organization.

This approach represents a profound shift in administrative thought and practice. Traditionally, superintendents were part of a top-down approach to professional learning by identifying so-called best practices and requiring all teachers to attend workshops and emulate those practices (Dickson & Mitchell, 2014). However, as the leader of learning role emerged, they realized that they had to shift away from the traditional role of control over professional learning.

Superintendents are beginning to recognize the need to align their own commitment to learning with the essential learning required of students, teachers, and principals. Their experience confirms Darling-Hammond and Richardson's (2009) argument that leaders should facilitate the creation of work-embedded professional learning opportunities that emerge naturally from actual student and teacher learning experiences.

An additional challenge for the modern superintendent is to effectively articulate the concept of the professional learning community to all stakeholders in the school community. This must include parents as changes will no doubt affect scheduling, curriculum design, and instructional delivery. Although the term "learning community" has become somewhat ubiquitous in today's educational lexicon, a universal understanding of this concept remains elusive. As Michael Fullan (2005) notes, "there is a growing problem in large-scale reform; namely, the terms travel well, but the underlying conceptualization and thinking do not."

This lack of conceptual clarity has led school leaders to mistakenly identify any team or meeting as a learning community, regardless of how the team was formed or its intended purpose. Some of these teams are not learning communities any more than when teachers turn students' desks together during instruction and call it cooperative learning. In fact, when teams or meetings have been mandated from above and use top-down methods to drive the agenda of the team or the purpose of the meeting, they represent the antithesis of authentic learning communities. Leithwood (2010) maintains that, under such circumstances, learning communities do not yield the expected transformation of instructional practices and improvement in student learning.

Concepts such as late starts or early releases to allow faculty to collaborate will impact family schedules. Differentiation, flipped classrooms, and other instructional innovations will likely invite parent interest and even concern. Ensuring that collaborative teams, the smaller elements of the larger learning community, meet, collaborate, and act on that collaboration will be critical to ensuring authentic work. The superintendent's role, as a true learning leader, will be to ensure that these activities thrive across the school organization and do not devolve into planning time by another name.

Truly effective superintendents understand that, at their core, they must be able to build and nurture cultures that build capacity for all to emerge as leaders and innovators. They recognize that the greatest loyalty and strongest levels of commitment flow to the smallest part of the organization because that is where people's engagement levels are the highest. They are wise enough to recognize that the greatest loyalty is to the smallest team, and that it is at the team level that teachers realize the greatest opportunity for engagement, dialogue, and decision-making (DuFour et al., 2010).

A Study of School Leader Core Competencies

Based on the review of literature on leader core competencies, the Educational Leadership Constituent Council (ELCC), the Professional Standards for Educational Leaders (PSEL), and the author's own experience, a list of school leader core competencies was created. A study based on these core competencies was also conducted. The purpose of the study was to obtain the opinions of current public school leaders (superintendents and principals) to determine the most-valued core competencies for these positions.

The research questions for this study were:

1. What are the most important core competencies for superintendents of public schools?
2. What are the most important core competencies for principals in public schools?
3. Is there a significant difference in the importance of the core competencies between superintendents and school principals?

The participants in this study consisted of forty-two K–12 public school leaders which included sixteen public school superintendents and twenty-six public school principals in selected elementary and secondary schools in northeast Illinois. The respondents held school leadership positions in

Chicago-area suburban school districts. They were defined as school leaders working full-time in the official role of either superintendent or principal. The participants came from diverse economic, cultural, ethnic, gender, and academic backgrounds.

A two-part questionnaire was used in this study. Part one consisted of a list of the twelve core competencies in which the respondents were asked to rate the competencies based upon their importance for performing the job of superintendent or principal (see figure 3.1). The survey instrument consisted of twelve core competencies that were validated through a series of expert reviews.

The twelve school leader core competencies were also linked to the ELCC and the PSEL (see figure 3.2). Each of the core competencies was mapped with these standards based upon degree of association. All core competencies were covered within the standards and there appeared to be comprehensive coverage.

The second part consisted of an open-ended question that asked the respondents to describe any other core competencies that were important for a superintendent or principal serving in public schools. Respondents were also given additional space for other comments. In some cases, follow-up interviews were conducted with the respondents to gain further information concerning the core competencies and responsibilities of the positions.

The idea of clarifying core competencies is not new but has received increasing attention in the wake of growing accountability and legislative reform. This is particularly true as districts come to grips with both identifying specific competencies desirable in superintendents and recognizing that when superintendents are not successful, it can come at great cost to the district. More importantly, school boards and superintendent preparation programs

	Core Competencies	Descriptions
1.	School governance	Collaborating and working with district school board members.
2.	School law	Understanding laws impacting district leadership and operations.
3.	Instructional leadership	Being a proactive, involved leader in improving district instruction.
4	Resource management	Managing financial, facility, and human resources and regulations.
5.	Vision leadership	Leading and motivating staff for improved performance of school initiatives.
6.	Change leadership	Leading and managing school change and improvements.
7.	Communication	Communicating to school district staff and stakeholders.
8.	Strategic planning	Developing and setting educational goals.
9.	School data management	Interpreting and using school data and assessment information.
10.	Community relations	Developing and working with school community members, parents, etc.
11.	Diverse learner strategies	Providing effective instruction for diverse students.
12.	Collaboration	Building collaboration and teamwork.

Figure 3.1.   Core competencies of school leaders.

School Leader Core Competencies	ELCC Standards	PSEL Standards
School governance	1, 4, 6, 7	1, 4, 5, 6
School law	5, 6, 7	5, 6
Instructional leadership	1, 4, 6, 7	1, 4, 6
Resource management	3, 5, 6, 7	3, 5, 6
Vision leadership	1, 2, 4, 5	1, 2, 4, 5
Change leadership	1, 4, 6	1, 4, 6
Communication	1, 3, 4, 6, 7	1, 3, 4, 6
Strategic planning	1, 2, 4, 6, 7	1, 2, 4, 6
School data management	1, 2, 4, 5, 6	1, 2, 4, 5, 6
Community relations	1, 4, 6, 7	1, 4, 6
Diverse learner strategies	1, 2, 4, 5, 6	1, 2, 4, 5, 6
Collaboration	1, 3, 4, 5, 7	1, 3. 4, 5

Figure 3.2.   Comparison of the school leader core competencies and ELCC and PSEL standards.

will need to identify the technical core of the superintendent's work in order to optimize their readiness and performance. Researchers can also help craft effective tools to link school superintendents with the technical core of their profession and reinforce a school administration's knowledge base so that the professional learning community model can produce greater student achievement, deeper learning, and greatness as an expectation embedded in the twenty-first-century school.

It can be argued that for more than a decade, four questions remain at the center of the discussion and drive conversation about superintendent preparation and the identification of core competencies:

1. Are instructional programs and student learning a result of school superintendent's skills in organizing staff and allocating financial resources?
2. Do NCATE (National Council for Accreditation of Teacher Evaluation) [CAEP (Council for the Accreditation of Educator Preparation)], AASA (American Association of School Administrators), and PSEL (Professional Standards for Educational Leaders) standards-driven preparation programs produce superintendents with superior instructional leadership skills and dispositions?
3. What skills and leadership dispositions propel some superintendents toward greater success than others in improving instruction and student performance?

4. Do leadership practices of school superintendents, as measured by Leadership Practices Inventory (LPI) by James Kouzes and Barry Posner, and other self-report leadership measures, relate to the quality of instruction and student performance (Achilles, 2001)?

This survey offered in this book is yet another attempt to push that conversation forward and clarify the definition of the core competencies essential to service as a school superintendent in the twenty-first century.

Definitions for the core competencies were created to assist the respondents in defining each of the core competencies (see figure 3.1). In some cases, interviews were conducted with teacher leaders in helping to clarify the core competencies and definitions. A standard Likert scale (5 = most important and 1 = least important) was used. Also, the scale included the option of "0" indicating that the teacher leaders found the core competency to be irrelevant given they did not have job responsibilities in that area.

The survey instrument included identification of two types of school leaders—superintendents and principals. Respondents were asked to identify themselves as either a superintendent or school principal. All the respondents were acting in a full-time capacity and had no direct teaching responsibilities.

There were several limitations of the study that included nonrandom selection, low and disproportionate sample numbers, and the lack of differentiation of the school district core mission, and grade level (e.g., elementary or high school). All the respondents who were asked to complete the survey were very cooperative and helpful in providing opinions about their jobs and their overall roles and responsibilities in public schools.

The core competencies of all groups were rank-ordered using descriptive statistics, and significant differences were calculated using a two-sample test of significance. The narrative comments were typed verbatim and compiled in each of the core competencies. All responses were kept anonymous and the original survey instruments were destroyed to further protect the identity of the respondents.

The results of the study for the superintendents indicated that they ranked the top core competencies as: school governance (4.86), collaboration (4.80), vision leadership (4.52), strategic planning (4.47), community relations (4.46), and instructional leadership (4.61) (see table 3.1). The core competencies that were least valued for a superintendent included: change leadership (4.50), communication (4.49), resource management (4.20), school law (4.01), school data management (3.94), and diverse learner strategies (3.90) (see table 3.1).

These rankings were consistent with several of the comments in the second part of the questionnaire and interviews. Respondents commented that work-

Table 3.1.   **Rank Order of Superintendent Core Competencies.**

Core Competencies	Mean
1. School governance	4.86
2. Collaboration	4.80
3. Vision leadership	4.52
4. Strategic planning	4.47
5. Instructional leadership	4.61
6. Community relations	4.46
7. Change leadership	4.50
8. Communication	4.49
9. Resource management	4.20
10. School law	4.01
11. School data management	3.94
12. Diverse learner strategies	3.90

ing with school boards was of critical importance. Some commented that they believed the role of the superintendent is to teach the board regarding issues facing the school district and that, in the best districts, the relationship between superintendent and the board is a hybrid relationship often moving between professional, personal, and political.

Other respondents warned that too often superintendents speak the language of collaboration but fail to follow up to ensure that all are actively engaged in the collaborative effort. They noted that in a perfect world, all would embrace the collaborative model. But, embedding measures of accountability, especially in the emerging stages of the professional learning community (PLC) model, is critical to it being successful. One principal spoke plainly on this topic saying, "What is not monitored becomes optional." Another was more hopeful and indicated that once the school passed through the "emerging" stage of the PLC model, then effective practice became, "who we are, not what we do."

Many principals and superintendents had strong feelings about the political nature of school leadership. Comments such as "keep your friends close and your enemies closer," "trust but verify," and even "trust in God but everyone else must bring data" were not uncommon in conversations with respondents. In particular, veteran superintendents felt the need to be very politically astute and were fond of pointing out that board support was often short-lived. One even went so far as to say that, "superintendents begin to lose their job the day they get it."

A very common conversational theme with principals, superintendents, and interestingly enough, many new and emerging leaders, was the need for superintendents to passionately articulate a clear vision and plan for the school organization; "to motivate, inspire, and lead from the front." It also provoked comments about their wish for more specific training on how to develop the ability to do so.

The core competencies that were most valued by the principals for a principal position included: change leadership (4.88), vision leadership (4.80), collaboration (4.76), strategic planning (4.72), communication (4.60), and diverse learner strategies (4.46). The core competencies that were least valued included: community relations (4.44), instructional leadership (4.24), school data management (4.21), resource management (4.10), school law (4.08), and school governance (3.48) (see table 3.2).

While the rankings of the school leaders (superintendents and principals) were somewhat similar, there were two core competencies that were statistically significant. The first one was school board governance ($p < .01$). The superintendents ranked this core competency as the most valued for the superintendent position ($\mu = 4.86$). The principals ranked this core competency as the last for a principal position ($\mu = 3.48$). This might be explained because the superintendents need to work very closely with their boards while principals do so with less frequency.

Another core competency that was statistically significant was understanding diverse learning. The superintendents ranked this core competency last ($\mu = 3.90$). The principals value this core competency much more and ranked it number six ($\mu = 4.46$). This ranking difference might be explained by the fact that principals are in more direct daily contact with teachers and staff in educating diverse learners and need to be proficient themselves. See table 3.3.

For superintendents in districts with rapidly changing demographics, these data should serve as a wake-up call. The effective twenty-first-century

Table 3.2.   Rank Order of Principal Core Competencies.

Core Competencies	Mean
1. Change leadership	4.88
2. Vision leadership	4.80
3. Collaboration	4.76
4. Strategic planning	4.72
5. Communication	4.60
6. Diverse learner strategies	4.46
7. Community relations	4.44
8. Instructional leadership	4.24
9. School data management	4.21
10. Resource management	4.10
11. School law	4.08
12. School governance	3.48

Table 3.3.   Comparison of Core Competencies between Superintendents
and Principals.

	Superintendent			Principal		
Core Competencies	Mean	Med	S.D.	Mean	Med	S.D.
School governance	**4.86	5	.61	3.48	3	.96
School law	4.01	4	.65	4.08	4	.88
Instructional leadership	4.46	4	.54	4.24	4	.83
Resource management	4.20	4	.41	4.10	4	.57
Vision leadership	4.52	4	.64	4.80	5	.41
Change leadership	4.50	5	.73	4.88	5	.33
Communication	4.40	4	.82	4.60	5	.61
Strategic planning	4.47	4	.74	4.72	5	.45
School data management	3.94	4	.59	4.21	4	.67
Community relations	4.61	4	.63	4.44	5	.76
Diverse learner strategies	*3.90	4	.71	4.46	4	.51
Collaboration	4.80	5	.41	4.76	5	.45

*$p<.05$; **$p<.01$; n=16(s) and 26(p)

superintendent can no longer afford to be uninformed about strategies for serving diverse learners. Much like teachers, superintendents, and principals, all levels of leadership in the district will need to closely collaborate on how best to meet the needs of those learners traditionally underrepresented and underserved in our schools.

This study indicates that helping all school leaders to develop these core competencies can be beneficial. The need for authentic, practical leadership training cannot be overstated. To achieve this end however, the modern superintendent has an ethical, moral, and professional responsibility to commit the school organization to offering meaningful professional leader development opportunities for both building leaders and emerging leaders as well. Too often, these opportunities are squandered because professional development funds are allocated elsewhere.

The core competencies, as shown in this study, seem to offer a way out of the wilderness, however. They offer concrete application in the context of two sets of standards. More importantly, the idea that a paradigm shift is occurring is borne out by the rankings of these competencies. Both principals and superintendents rank collaboration, instructional leadership, vision, and strategic planning in the top half of the competencies with the more traditional competencies in the lower half of the rankings.

What this may suggest is that the paradigm which placed high value on the more traditional managerial competencies is being replaced by those that impact culture; a culture that moves away from a teaching school toward that of a learning school. It suggests also that the concept of fostering collaborative, professional learning community cultures is becoming embedded in the mindset of current and emerging leaders.

If that is true, it may lead to the next evolution of the professional learning community model. Returning to the idea that the greatest loyalty is to the smallest team, visionary superintendents may finally be able to redefine the next evolution of the professional learning community model that will be known as the intentional learning community. The school as intentional learning community, a learning organization, folds all adult energy and practice into student mastery of knowledge and most importantly, skills to apply that knowledge.

It can even be argued that the rankings indicate that an emerging contrast between old school and new school thinking may be taking hold as illustrated in figure 3.3.

While there are some anomalies in the competency rankings, such as school governance and diverse learner strategies, there seems to be a clear prioritization of core competencies that indicates a shift to culture-oriented leadership, one that that recognizes the need for a more strategic, even systemic, reframing of schools as true learning organizations (Senge, 2006).

With increasing frequency, literature on school organizational change is expanding its treatment of systemic school improvement. There is, or should be, an increasing crossover of private sector organizational change theory and

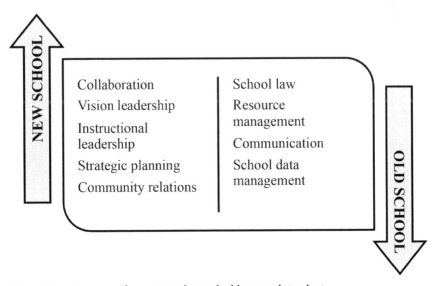

Figure 3.3.   Contrast of competencies ranked by superintendents.

practice into public sector change research and practice, particularly in public education. Unfortunately, there has been a long-held belief that public education had nothing to learn from private sector organizational theory. However, success stories like Google, Starbucks, GE, Southwest Airlines, Walgreens, Tesla, Amazon, and IBM illustrate that these companies are, at their core, organizations of individuals learning from each other through reflection on best practice. Like their private sector counterparts, school districts are, or should be, learning organizations comprised of individuals working collaboratively toward commonly agreed-upon goals.

Leaders of learning organizations, both corporate chief executive officers and superintendents, guide a shared vision of exemplary performance, manage disparate components and constituents to ensure progress toward goals, and serve as a model for inspired leadership. Corporate and school executive leaders personify the aspirations and responsibilities of the entire organization (DiPaola & Stronge, 2003).

Barnard (2013) argues that "in effect, schools have to unlearn the false rationale of separatist, component, tool-box thinking if they are to prevent old ideas and assumptions from hitching a ride on the old road to school improvement." So, given the demonstrated success of the professional learning community model and if deployed in the context of the twelve core competencies, what might be the next step for the twentieth-first-century superintendent?

FUSION LEADERSHIP AND THE THIRD WAY

The twelve core competencies in this study provide a valuable framework for building leadership capacity in the aspiring superintendent. It is useful, then, to also examine the cultural context of the district that might further enhance the superintendent's growth as a true leader of learners. As with most everything else in public education, the research on school cultures has evolved. Over the nearly a century-and-a-half, leaders and reformers of American public education have driven three major cultural shifts, or "ways" of adapting to challenges from internal and external forces. Figure 3.4 illustrates the evolution of those school cultures.

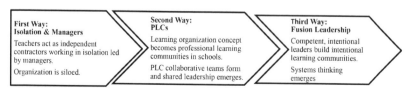

Figure 3.4.   The evolution of school cultures.

For much of the nineteenth and twentieth century, the First Way of adapting the school culture was to allow, even authorized, teachers to work largely in isolation, primarily supervised by managerial leaders. Superintendents managed principals who in turn managed teachers who managed students. Accountability focused on everything but student learning and achievement. Textbooks defined curriculum, instruction, and assessment.

In the later twentieth century, a Second Way of looking at cultural reform began to emerge. The idea of the learning organization, drawn most notably from the work of Peter Senge's *The Fifth Discipline* (1990/2006), helped to launch conversations across the education profession regarding the potential values of using teaming as a way to implement change. This learning organizational model mimicked cultural shifts in manufacturing and industry where reformers and innovators effectively, and profitably, mirrored their European and Asian counterparts who had already capitalized on smarter ways to use teams of competent workers, professionals, and leaders to increase quality and productivity.

As schools began to reexamine more collaborative models, the idea of the professional learning community continued to evolve. Schools moved steadily toward organizing teachers into collaborative teams that worked toward commonly agreed-upon goals while holding each other mutually accountable for the collective work of the team. The professional learning community model in schools became fully formed in the mid-1990s.

For nearly twenty years, the professional learning community school model has experienced consistent success in meeting the demand and challenges of increased accountability for student achievement produced by the series of legislative reforms and stakeholder pressure. Schools using the collaborative model tend to improve. Collaboration focused around best practices for learning works.

While many different versions of the professional learning community model have evolved, many local models have been miscommunicated by leaders and misunderstood by staff. This has resulted in a steady drifting away from the intent and design of the original model. That being said, the question for the next generation of superintendents who embrace the twelve core competencies in this study is: how might superintendents reinvent and redefine the cultural context of professional learning community models to allow districts to move to an even greater level of success?

By demonstrating proficiency in the twelve competencies as an intentional leader, superintendents can move to a Third Way by creating the next generation of professional learning communities represented by the emergence of an intentional learning community. The concept of intentional leader and the intentional learning community derives its name from the concept of intentional teaching, which is defined as teaching that happens deliberately, with intent, and does not happen by chance. It is reflectively planned, thoughtful, and purposeful. Intentional teachers use their knowledge, judgment, and expertise to organize learning experiences for children; when an unplanned situation arises (as it always does), they can recognize a teaching opportunity and take advantage of it, too (Epstein, 2015).

To be intentional is to act purposefully, with a goal in mind, and a plan for accomplishing it. The intentional learning community consistently maintains a laser-beam focus on the four critical questions (see chapter 2). Intentional teaching acts originate from careful thought. So it is with intentional leadership. It is also purposeful, exemplified by intentional acts originating from careful thought and competent practice. It has strategic goals in mind and a specific and smart plan for accomplishing them. It is focused and relentless in pursuit of goals and positive student outcomes.

Systems thinking embraced by intentional leaders in an intentional learning community rounds out the concept of fusion leadership or the Third Way. Figure 3.5 illustrates this idea.

The idea of systems thinking is not new. It is based on the principle that each organization is composed of a system of interrelated processes and people which make up the system's components. The success of all workers within the system is dependent on the leader's capability to orchestrate

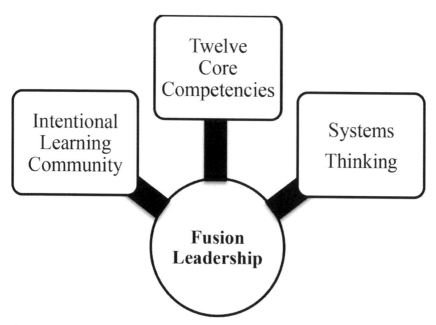

Figure 3.5. Components of fusion leadership.

the delicate balance of each component for optimization of the entire system (Berry, 2011). John Seddon (2008) takes it one step further:

> If investment . . . has not been matched by improvement, it is because we have invested in the wrong things. We invest in the wrong things believing them to be the right things. We think inspection drives improvement. We believe in the notion of economies of scale. We think choice and quasi-markets are levers for improvement. We believe people can be motivated by incentives. We think leaders need vision, managers need targets, and information technology is a driver of change. These are all wrong-headed ideas. But they have been the foundation of public sector "reform."

The effective twenty-first-century superintendent will use systems thinking not only to optimize the performance of every aspect of the school organization but also as a countermeasure to the problems so often emblematic of public school organizations. These problems include:

- Things never quite work as predicted, resulting in a range of unforeseeable consequences.
- Information is lost in the system or is not accessible, causing reworking and delays.
- Misunderstandings arise among school stakeholders, leading to mistakes.
- Information needed is rarely complete, so people operate with best-bet assumptions.
- Work is skimped and dodged, and cheating occurs, but the school carries on regardless.
- Job specifications become overly complex, causing work difficulties and group silos to develop (Barnard, 2013).

The use of systems thinking is a revolutionary paradigm shift for public schools and their leadership but one that is long overdue. The triad of fusion leadership, or the Third Way, offers a compelling vision of how twenty-first-century school superintendents can lead our schools into the future.

Fusion leadership demands that superintendents go beyond traditional definitions of district leadership. It demands mastery of the twelve core competencies by an intentional leader, within a thriving, intentional learning community, using systems thinking as the organizational change model to achieve authentic, sustainable school improvement.

SUMMARY

This study offers some hopeful implications as the role of the modern and effective superintendent shifts focus from traditional district leader to a true leader of learning. A focus on the core competencies in this study offers hope that current and emerging leaders alike recognize the linkage between the power of culture, the need for creating intentional learning communities, and the superintendent as the learning leader of those communities.

Educational literature contains many examples of studies outlining the roles, responsibilities, capacities, and traits of school leaders. For this study, the twelve core competencies were identified as school governance, school law, instructional leadership, resource management, vision leadership, change leadership, communication, strategic planning, school data management, community relations, diverse learner strategies, and collaboration. Principals, superintendents, and school leadership candidates were asked to rate each as to its importance in their particular position. Some of the ratings were not surprising while others provoked some interesting and revealing information.

When examined as a whole, however, it is interesting to note an emerging emphasis on vision, collaboration, strategic planning, and instructional leadership, especially among superintendents. The rankings by superintendents may indicate that they are beginning to view the role of the superintendent differently. Several superintendents indicated as much and felt this resulted from greater accountability, legislative reforms, and their own positive experience as leaders using new and innovative organizational change models. Anecdotal comments by principals and emerging leaders reflected a desire to see greater collaboration between superintendents and building leaders and for authentic collaboration between all elements of the school organization in order to "multiply" the talent, knowledge, and skill of all involved in the work of the school and district.

Fusion leadership then, offers intentional leaders a Third Way to integrate the twelve core competencies into an intentional learning community using a systems thinking organizational model.

CASE STUDY

You are a new superintendent of a large suburban high school district. During your interview for the position, the board of education expressed concern regarding the lack of true collaboration across the high school. They felt that most teachers work largely in isolation and that this is, in part, the reason why standardized test scores have remained flat for years. Not only have annual standardized test scores remained flat, the board of education believes that staff has accepted a culture of mediocrity as the norm or status quo and that the current school culture reflects an attitude of "good enough is good enough."

The board also felt that under the last superintendent, there was very little faculty and staff accountability for student performance and overall professionalism. The last superintendent attempted to institute a professional learning community model but as you speak with faculty and staff, it is clear that there is very little understanding of how the model works. Explain, in detail, how you will effect a "culture shift." In particular, how will you foster a clear understanding of the PLC model, and what specific actions will you take to implement the PLC model?

EXERCISES AND DISCUSSION QUESTIONS

1. In your early days as superintendent, you come to understand two things about the union in your district. First, the union is very strong and has had significant influence on the former superintendent regarding both policy and administrator evaluation. Second, under the previous superintendent, your assistant superintendent for curriculum and supervision closely aligned herself with union leadership. Your building leaders are telling you that this relationship is ongoing and has impacted decisions about curriculum, instruction, and assessment. What will be your first steps in addressing this situation?

2. The parents in your community are upset and have recently organized around the issue of the role of athletics in your district. Many of the parents feel there is too much emphasis given to academic achievement and not enough attention given to athletic opportunities for students. The parents are demanding that an athletic improvement committee be created to seek ways to expand and enhance the athletic opportunities for students in the district. Explain how you will address this issue and what your response will be to the demands of the parents.

3. The board of education has given you a directive to investigate upgrades to the technology in your district. They are especially interested in new technologies to be used to enhance instruction. Two of your board members are executives of technology-provider companies and are very knowledgeable. Your faculty has many older members who are resistant to new technology. Explain how you will approach this directive and specifically, describe your action steps to improving key stakeholders in the process.

4. During your first six months as superintendent of a K–8 district and despite your best efforts to be a learning leader in the district, you are discovering that most of your time is being consumed by managing the general operations of the district. As the year comes to an end you are resolved to make changes to ensure that more of your time in the coming year will be dedicated to more direct involvement with teaching and learning. What are some of the steps you will take to ensure this happens and that you will become the learning leader you aspire to be?

REFERENCES

Achilles, C. (2001). What is missing in the current debate about educational adminis-tration? (EDAD) standards. *The AASA Professor, 24*(2), 8–14.

Barnard, P. (2013). *The systems thinking school: Redesigning schools from the inside out.* Lanham, MD: Rowman & Littlefield Education.

Berry, B. (2011). There is a relationship between systems thinking and W. Edwards Deming's theory of profound knowledge. *The Berrywood Group*. Retrieved from http://www.berrywood.com/wp-content/uploads/2011/08/demingpaper.pdf.

Bredeson, P., & Kose, B. W. (2007). Responding to the education reform agenda: A study of school superintendents' instructional leadership. *Education Policy Analy-sis Archives, 15*(5). Retrieved from http://epaa.asu.edu/ojs/article/view/53.

Cuban, L. (1988). *The managerial imperative and the practice of leadership in schools.* Albany: State University of New York Press.

Darling-Hammond, L., & Richardson, N. (2009). Teacher learning: What matters? *Educational Leadership, 66*(5), 46–53.

Dickson, J., & Mitchell, C. (2014, May 8). Shifting the role: School-district super-intendents' experiences as they build a learning community. *Canadian Journal of Educational Administration Policy, 158*, 21. Retrieved from https://www.umani toba.ca/publications/cjeap/pdf_files/dickson_mitchell.pdf.

DiPaola, M. F., & Stronge, J. (2003). *Superintendent evaluation handbook.* Lanham, MD: Scarecrow.

DuFour, R., DuFour, R., Eaker, R., & Many, T. (2010). *Learning by doing: A hand-book for professional communities at work. A practical guide for PLC teams and leadership.* Bloomington, IN: Solution Tree Press.

Epstein, A. (2015). Introducing intentional teaching. *Intentional teacher: Choos-ing the best strategies for young children's learning.* Retrieved from http://www.highscope.org/ProductCart/pc/catalog/SamplePagesTOC/Intentional%20 Teacher2_Sample.pdf.

Fullan, M. (2005). *Leadership and sustainability.* Thousand Oaks, CA: Corwin Press.

Gehrman, E. (2008). Building a new structure for school leadership: With account-ability standards creating more public scrutiny than ever before, educational lead-ers must focus their efforts on instruction. Based on essay by Elmore, R. (2004). Building a new structure for school leadership. In *School reform from the inside out: Policy, practice, and performance.* Cambridge, MA: Harvard Education Press. Retrieved from https://www.gse.harvard.edu/news/uk/08/05/building-new-structure -school-leadership.

Kowalski, T. (2005). Evolution of the school district superintendent position. *Edu-cational Leadership Faculty Publications, 26.* eCommons: University of Dayton. Retrieved from http://ecommons.udayton.edu/eda_fac_pub/26/.

Leithwood, K. (2010, February). *How the Leading Student Achievement project im-proves student learning: An evolving theory of action* [Report to the Ministry of Education of Ontario]. Retrieved from http://resources.curriculum.org/LSA/files/ LSA TheoryofAction.pdf.

Murphy, J. (1990). Principal instructional leadership. In L. S. Lotto and P. W. Thurston (Eds.), *Advances in educational administration: Changing perspectives on the school, I, Part B* (pp. 163–200). Greenwich, CT: JAI Press.

Seddon, J. (2008). *Systems thinking in the public sector: The failure of the reform regime and a manifesto for a better way.* Station Yard, UK: Triarchy Press.

Senge, P. (1990/2006). *The fifth discipline: The art and practice of the learning organization.* New York: Random House.

Chapter Four

Policy and Politics

The Superintendent as CEO

OBJECTIVES

At the conclusion of this chapter you will be able to:

1. Describe the purpose of a school board (ELCC 6; PSEL 3, 4, 5, 8, 9, 10).
2. Identify potential conflicts between the board and the superintendent (ELCC 5, 6; PSEL 1, 2, 3, 4, 6, 9, 10).
3. Describe the role of policy and politics in district governance (ELCC 1, 2, 5, 6; PSEL 1–10).
4. Describe community involvement in district policy and governance (ELCC 1, 2, 3, 6; PSEL 8, 9).
5. Identify how policies and politics impact the needs of students (ELCC 1, 2, 5; PSEL 1, 3, 4, 5, 8, 9).

THE ROLE OF SCHOOL BOARDS IN PUBLIC EDUCATION

Why do we need school boards? After all, the experts are the professionally trained educators, right? Why should lay people who are not trained in education have oversight of schools? The answer lies in the word "public" in public schools. This refers to the fact that it is the citizens themselves who control schools. In most states, depending on the size and configuration of the district, they do this by electing a school board of three, five, or seven members who must be residents of the school district.

According to recent data from the U.S. Department of Education, school boards govern the overwhelming majority of the approximately 13,600 public school districts in America and they make up fully one-sixth of all the local

57

governments in the country (U.S. Department of Education, *Digest of Education Statistics 2012,* table 216.20, cited in 2013 publication). School boards also retain broad popular support. They are how citizens have been accustomed to seeing their school districts governed for the past century and the means through which parents and community members gain access to school policies and services.

Local control over education forms a core value in the foundation of our nation. To understand the potential influence of local school boards, it is important to look at their authority within the context of state and federal education policy. Dating back to the founding of our nation, public education has been the responsibility of the state. This function was granted through the Tenth Amendment to the United States Constitution.

This amendment states, "The powers not delegated to the United States by the Constitution, nor prohibited by it to the States, are reserved to the States respectively, or to the people" (U.S. Constitution, amendment X). Since education is not mentioned in the Constitution, it is one of those powers reserved to the states. Thus, states have plenary, or absolute, power in the area of education.

In turn, states have delegated this responsibility to locally elected school boards charged with overseeing the operations of specific schools. Over time, this responsibility has evolved to the oversight of clusters of schools organized under the administrative umbrella of central district offices guided by state-specific education policies and codes, which are also influenced and governed by federal statutes. It is not surprising that elected school boards are a legacy of our origins as a nation.

Supporters of this governance model see local school boards as an essential reflection of our commitment to representative democratic government and local control. Yet, there are contemporary critics and politicians who dislike them and see them as a hindrance to both equity and quality in education. Critics cite a history of low expectations, inequitable funding, and segregation by race and economic status as evidence that local control can lead to organizations that do not reflect our broader national values or commitment to equal opportunity for all citizens. It is a primary reason why the federal government has taken a more active role in public education over the past several decades.

Beginning in the 1960s, and building on arguments made in *Brown v. Board of Education* in 1954, the federal government began playing an increasing role in public education through federal legislation and categorical funding such as the Elementary and Secondary Education Act of 1965 (ESEA) amended in 2011, and the Education for All Handicapped Children Act of 1975 (EHCA). Both of these laws were designed to provide resources to students marginalized in school systems largely due to policies developed by state and local school boards (e.g., policies that segregated students by race, disability, income, or funding that led to substantial inequities).

Subsequent Congressional reauthorizations of ESEA, EHCA, the Individuals with Disabilities Education Act of 1997 (IDEA), the No Child Left Behind Act of 2001 (NCLB), and the Every Student Succeeds Act (ESSA) made federal law on December 10, 2015 continue to further expand the role of the federal government in public education. These federal laws expand and support a longstanding commitment of the federal government to equal opportunity for all students. These Acts make funding available to districts to provide additional support for specific groups of students (e.g., students with disabilities and students living in poverty).

POLICY, SCHOOL BOARDS, AND THE SUPERINTENDENT

The influential NCLB and ESSA and associated regulations are intended to target persistently low-performing schools. They also support initiatives such as the Common Core State Standards aimed at ensuring that all states strive to teach a high-level curriculum and administer rigorous assessments. Under these conditions, with local control seemingly eroded by more and more federal oversight, what then is the evolving role of the school board and that of the superintendent? The National School Boards Association (NSBA) states that, "School board members serve their local communities as stewards of public trust charged with making decisions that ensure all students have access to high quality learning experiences in efficient and well managed environments" (National School Boards Association, 2011, p. 2).

The NSBA developed a framework of eight critical areas called the "work of school boards" that boards may adopt in order to be effective in improving student achievement. While not intended to be addressed in any specific priority order, NSBA suggests the areas are to be considered and implemented as a whole to create optimal conditions for student success. As boards do their work, one very important function is to successfully recruit and hire a superintendent who guides the school board with their key work. See figure 4.1 for the NSBA's key work of school boards.

A foundation for the key work of school boards is called policy. Policies are principles adopted by school boards to chart a course of action. They may include why and how much is needed for the initiatives taken. Policies should be broad enough to indicate the procedures to be followed by the administration in meeting a number of problems and narrow enough to give clear guidance. Policies are guides for action by the superintendent, who then

- Identify vision and mission
- Develop standards for performance
- Support assessment of performance
- Implement accountability for performance
- Align resources to support performance
- Prioritize climate and culture
- Develop collaborative relationships and engage community
- Commit to continuous improvement

Figure 4.1.   Framework for key work of school boards. (National School Boards Association, 2011.)

implements the rules and regulations to provide specific direction to school personnel for accountability of the policy implementation.

Boards develop policies and put them in writing so that they may serve as guidelines and goals for the successful and efficient functioning of the public schools. Most school boards consider policy development their chief function, along with providing the guidelines for actions concerning personnel, buildings, resources, and equipment for the successful administration, application, and execution of their policies. Policies serve as sources of information and guidance for all people who are interested in, or connected with, the public schools.

Policies of school boards should be framed, and interpreted, in terms of rules and regulations of the state boards of education, and all other regulatory agencies within county, state, and federal levels of government. A sample policy development process which a school board may adopt and use to formulate guidelines and structure for the governance of the schools under its jurisdiction can be seen in figure 4.2.

Policy Development Process

1. A policy change or need is identified. Required changes or an additional policy may be noted by the following:
   a. Board (including approved board resolutions and/or board committee recommendations).

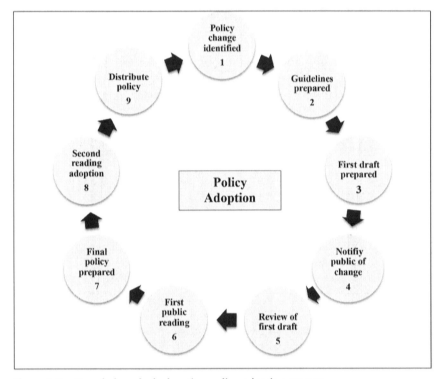

Figure 4.2.   Sample board of education policy adoption process.

   b. Superintendent.

   c. Legal requirement or mandate.

2. Superintendent prepares abstract of policy development guidelines. This defines issues and suggests approaches to be taken.

    If one exists, a board subcommittee charged with policy development reviews potential policy development guidelines. This subcommittee may suggest a position on issues; agrees on scope; establishes policy priority schedule and implementation guidelines.

3. Superintendent prepares first draft. Legal counsel is consulted if necessary.

4. Public announcement or notification of a proposed new or revised policy as an agenda item in a regularly scheduled board of education meeting.

5. Board presents and reviews draft during a board working session.

6. Board reviews draft at first reading in a regularly scheduled public meeting. Board members agree on substance; suggest wording change, if necessary.

7. Superintendent prepares final policy document.
8. Board takes action to adopt the policy at second reading in regularly scheduled board meeting.
9. An approved/adopted policy is distributed by the superintendent.

In most districts, the superintendent is directed to establish and maintain an orderly plan for preserving newly adopted policies and making them accessible to employees of the school district, to members of the board, and to the community at large. It is now common practice that an updated board of education operating policy manual is kept in electronic format through the district's web page. Also a copy of the updated policy manual is normally filed with the state commissioner or superintendent of education. As policies are added, deleted, or amended, a notice of each policy is kept on file on the district Web site and a copy filed with the state education office.

It is common practice that at least every two (2) years, a board will review its policies for the purpose of passing, revising, or deleting policies mandated by changing conditions. Boards should evaluate how the school staff has implemented policies. The board should rely on the school staff, students, and the community to provide evidence of the effect of the policies adopted. The superintendent is given the responsibility of calling to the board's attention all policies that need revision.

The following criteria may be used when evaluating policies for possible revision or updating as needed as required by law or mandate:

- Is the policy within the scope of the board's discretionary authority granted by state codes and statutes?
- Is the policy consistent with state and federal law and with the provisions of the U.S. Constitution or existing federal statutes?
- Does the policy have a legitimate purpose that is educationally valid, and/ or has a desirable end or objective?
- Does the policy reflect sound judgment and wisdom?
- Is the policy in the best interests of children and adults?
- Legal counsel should always be sought when in the opinion of the superintendent or the board a question exists regarding the legality of a policy.

POLICIES, POLITICS, AND THE SCHOOL BOARD

Policies are essential to the efficient operation of a district. Yet the politics of the community affect board policies and the efficient operation of a board, the superintendent, and the school district. It is important to identify two important principles concerning school boards as they affect school and district leaders working with these boards. These principles are:

1. all district administrators are agents of the board of education and as such, are required to carry out board policy and procedures, and
2. all administrators must exhibit ethical behavior as they work with boards of education in efficient operation of the schools and district.

These statements may seem simplistic and obvious to any superintendent. However, these two principles are critical to the success of school board operations, district governance, and administrative performance. The three unknown dynamics influencing all parties are those of politics, control, and power.

Many issues drive the politics of local school districts and their boards. These influences could include but are not limited to: 1) level of community participation in school board elections both in terms of voter turnout and in terms of challengers to incumbent board members, 2) community demand for change influencing school board policies, 3) polarization and partisanship of community, county, and state politics leading to evidence of partisanship on school boards, and 4) board member personal agendas as reason to seek election to a school board.

For a theoretical foundation of the politics in community school boards, studies beginning in the 1970s cited the development of several theories of the role of school boards in making educational policy influenced by politics. These schools of thought, drawing on larger theories of democratic representation and politics, are summarized as dissatisfaction theory, continuous participation theory, decision-output theory, and public choice theory. See figure 4.3 for a brief description of each theory.

Dissatisfaction theory describes an electoral system with relative stability and little involuntary incumbent turnover punctuated by periods of extreme citizen dissatisfaction, contentious elections, and incumbent defeats (Iannaccone & Lutz, 1970; Lutz & Iannaccone, 2008). If one ignores nonpolitical cases of board turnover, such as voluntary retirements, poor health, or a family move out of the district, then dissatisfaction theory can generate some useful predictions. Alsbury (2008) makes the case that, in order to evaluate how responsive school board elections are to democratic forces, it is necessary to conduct a study of many districts over several electoral cycles. However, dissatisfaction theory provides very little insight into the motives of board members, superintendents, and voters.

Changing school board policy requires an inactive electorate to activate, challengers to run to replace incumbents in favor of the status quo, and a majority of board members to be defeated or change their positions in

Theory	Description	Key authors
Dissatisfaction	Long periods of stability in board elections interrupted by short periods of high turnover and participation.	Iannaccone and Lutz (1970, 2008)
Continuous Participation (Competition)	The small percentage of voters who continuously participate in board elections to have their preferences accurately reelected. Any spikes in participation are in line with the wishes of these groups.	Zeigler et al. (1974)
Decision-output (Responsiveness)	Undemocratic nature of school boards stems from the limited policy scope that board elections control, namely the public can only vote on local tax revenue and the policymakers on the board, who are constrained by federal and state policy.	Wirt and Kirst (1989)
Public Choice Theory	Challenges to incumbents arise based on policy choices of board members, voter preferences, and the expected payoffs associated with policy change.	Rada (1987, 1988) Moe (2011)

Figure 4.3.   Theories of school board politics.

response to the voter will. This most often leads to a change in the school district superintendent. Dissatisfaction theory does explain aggregate outcomes, such as turnover of school board members that leads to turnover of district superintendents. It does not explain the motives of candidates to run for the school board or of voters to vote for challengers, other than to say they do so out of dissatisfaction with the direction of the district. Thus, the political motives of board members, voters, and candidates are masked in such a theory.

Continuous participation theory argues that policies and political turnover in local districts is largely misleading. The basis of this theory argues that any changes in the makeup of the school board or in the school board policies represent a true change in the preferences of the 5 to 10 percent of the electorate who are constantly involved in educational policy at the local level. Spikes of participation may occur, but they are the direct result of the actions of this small group of active citizens. As a result, the decisions that result from such periods of greater participation are in line with the views of the citizens that have been engaged all along.

A study conducted by Moe (2011) researching educational policymaking at the local level by teachers unions can trace its roots to this theory. He argues that teachers unions function as a local interest group in educational policymaking, driving everything from school board candidate emergence, to voter turnout, to selection and replacement of district superintendents. Thus, when voter participation spikes or challenger candidates emerge, it is not a reflection of broad dissatisfaction within the community, but of a concentrated effort to activate the electorate on behalf of the goals of the local interest group.

A third theory, decision-output theory, is a derivative of continuous participation theory. It argues that educational policy at the local level is largely undemocratic. However, policy is undemocratic not because of capture of the system by a single interest group, but rather because the electoral inputs available to citizens allow them only to determine who makes public policy and how much local tax revenue to raise in support of schools (Wirt & Kirst, 1989).

Citizens are not able to truly determine education policy in these circumstances, but merely to determine the constraints within which educational policymakers must operate. In fact, it is the unelected and appointed district superintendent that dominates policymaking due to informational advantages and professional training. This often reduces the issue dimensions in a school board election to a single fiscal dimension. In such elections, the vote asking to raise tax levies and making new capital investments does not permit citizens to decide on the substantive content of the curriculum of study available to the students.

Finally, public choice theory is a later arrival to the study of school district governance. This theory borrows heavily from a rational choice background often viewed in economics and political science. In application to school boards, two types of school board members emerge, the power and/or the prestige candidate. Power candidates seek positions on the school board to change district policy and make decisions. Prestige candidates seek a position to fulfill civic duty or to gain notoriety within the community. Applying this single dimension (power or prestige) to board members generates a number of expectations about the emergence of different types of candidates, electoral challenges, and policy changes within a community.

All four of the theories have deep roots in political science literature. Understanding school boards provides an opportunity to evaluate what democratic policymaking looks like across a wide spectrum of citizen participation. While variations exist in state and federal congressional district elections, school board elections provide a much wider spectrum playing an influential and often contentious role in communities. Additionally, boards are an interesting test of candidate emergence. Entry to school board office is relatively inexpensive and most often completely free of party affiliations, unlike legislative office. It is why so many community members seek the office when, often, the only qualification they have is living within the school board boundaries.

Critics of school boards have a long and legitimate list of grievances. Turnout in school board elections is often quite low, making it easier for special interests (groups with single-focus ideological agendas or factions interested mostly in steering contracts to themselves and their friends) to get candidates elected. In many places, the very nature of school board politics seems to draw people with axes to grind, rather than motivated community leaders. There are many examples of communities where board members are in conflict with the district policies and politics. They're supposed to be setting policy for the school district, but they themselves are in conflict with each other and the policies they are attempting to disseminate.

Even when they are able to put ideology, partisanship, and personal gain aside, school boards often face an overwhelming set of challenges. They must deal with federal laws and state statutes concerning issues such as special education, homelessness, multilingual learners, and racial and ethnic reporting. There are federal court decisions on the rights of religious groups and the need to accommodate students with disabilities that influence the day-to-day operations of schools. Board members must make sure policies and operations meet federal and state laws when setting academic standards and balancing school budgets. While managing these federal and state requirements, there are local issues such as negotiations on union contracts that govern pay scales, class sizes, teacher assessment, and hiring and firing procedures.

All of these complex issues fall into the laps of school board members. That's in addition to the primary role of choosing and monitoring a superintendent, opening and closing schools, approving or disapproving charters, making decisions on buying or selling property, or formulating and then trying to sell bond measures to the voters. Effective district governance is not easy. It is time-consuming and can be a thankless job.

Into this mix, there are board members elected who often have no background in finance, administration, consensus building, political leadership, or even education. These are critical skills that the job of school board member practically demands. There are some states that require training for new members, but even then it is often cursory or quickly forgotten in the turmoil of meetings and decision-making. So the question is whether an elected or appointed board can do what is needed to manage the need for educational change.

POLICIES, POLITICS, AND THE COMMUNITY

No serious discussion of policies or accountability in schools can or should take place without community involvement. Perhaps more than any other governmental entity, school boards and their decisions directly influence a community's citizens. This role places boards of education, superintendents, building leaders, teachers, and support staff in a prime position to enlist the input and support of parents and community leaders on a variety of issues, including advancing a district's vision and mission. Community engagement and outreach requires that school boards carefully frame conversations about policies so everyone understands the purpose, rationale, and substance of public policy.

For instance, the building of new schools and the drawing or redrawing of attendance lines may elicit strong public sentiment and comment centering on the proposed board actions that affect personal interests. But this issue presents an opportunity for the board and superintendent to lead the community by shifting the conversation to one about student needs and program delivery as an educational value to the school district and the community.

When policies are well developed and effectively communicated, policies advance larger educational goals such as realizing higher student achievement, preparing students to be competitive in a global economy, and developing civic and democratic values. School boards must be clear about these larger goals, ensuring that district educators and community members fully understand the purpose and rationale behind any policy. This means helping the public understand that policies can be about providing academic and educational benefits to all students. Policies should recognize the uniqueness of a diverse student body, as well as acknowledge and celebrate student similarities and differences.

School boards and school leaders routinely engage the public in a variety of ways, and many of those avenues of communication are assets for carrying out the board's accountability role. Many districts conduct regular workshops and hearings with specific time slots on their agendas for citizen input. In fact, because state laws often govern local policymaking, many boards must conduct public hearings before policies are formally adopted. In policy development, boards often rely on citizen advisory committees, with members providing both lay and professional perspectives that can prove invaluable.

Community and business leaders are important voices in the discussion, often offering potential solutions that enrich the public debate and highlight the importance of diversity to the business community. Citizen advisory committees, especially when a school board is addressing controversial policy areas, can help reduce tensions and garner support.

Boards can employ various means to pursue district goals that are aligned with evidence-based educational outcomes. Conversations around issues will become part of the legal record. Considering a new or revised policy, such as a student assignment plan, requires a carefully deliberated process of evaluation. In other words, a board should "do its homework" to ensure the plan's success and sustainability. Ultimately, policies must be developed using a transparent process that is understood and followed by everyone.

Before establishing or refining a policy, a school board should gather relevant information about its context and history. This exercise may take weeks, months, or, for some large districts, even a year or two. Specifically, the board should examine district demographic information. This may include race and socioeconomic status, any governing court orders, relevant local or state laws, the educational effects of any current or previous policies, and political structures.

Also, a board should give substantial consideration to community values and interests. Public outreach can and should be informed by the background information collected, and school boards should anticipate criticisms by preparing persuasive responses and by considering public messaging. Finally, districts must periodically review and evaluate the design and operation of policies to ensure they are achieving the desired results. Periodic review is legally necessary for all policies, more so for policies that influence student learning and growth. Boards must ensure that their policies always reflect the educational goals of the district and those of the community.

Boards should hold public hearings and be receptive to public feedback from the community as well as from students and families. They should consider whether other design options would be as or more effective at achieving the district's goals, and document the board's rationale for discarding alternatives where appropriate.

A school board must ensure that the goals of any policy are reflected, complemented, and reinforced in the classrooms. Boards must work with schools to support their diverse student populations through curricular and extracurricular offerings and student services that create a culture in which student needs and differences are acknowledged and celebrated.

ACCOUNTABILITY AND THE SUPERINTENDENT

District leaders are heavily influenced by the politics of the board of education, the community, and the district they serve. They are legally and contractually bound to the policies and procedures of the board of education. Therefore, it is imperative that the district leader carefully study board policies and community politics. Equally important, they must understand and respect the values and culture of the community they serve. This may challenge a leader's personal beliefs and values. What is a superintendent to do?

First, the leader must have established a personal belief system built on a strong moral foundation. Secondly, the leader must have a clearly articulated conceptual framework built on relevant and principled leadership theories. This framework should reflect best practices in educational leadership and reflect high ethical standards of personal conduct. Not only must these standards be internalized in the leader, but they also must be evident in the day-to-day actions the leader takes in the district and school.

Leaders can get caught between what is practical and seemingly right in the circumstance, and a school board policy or procedure that may need changing or updating. But most often, leaders are simply caught in the micromanagement of board members who may have personal agendas. These personal agendas have a profound effect on and influence leader behaviors and actions.

For example, a school principal may be caught in a situation where a board member's child has violated the school district code of conduct. The superintendent must take required board policy action and administer the appropriate consequences. However, the board member intervenes and demands that the student action be ignored and/or dropped. Is it politically expedient to ignore the student behavior, or is it best to "let the chips fall where they may"?

Take for example, a case where parents, students, and community members challenge a board policy and administrative actions. For instance, a very popular baseball coach has been accused of poor behavior and possible student abuse. Board policy requires that the district and school leader investigate and take appropriate action for the student and the coach. In this case, the superintendent suspends the coach in question. There is outrage in the community, student protests, and a grievance filed by the union on behalf of the coach. What is the superintendent to do in this situation?

The case cannot be discussed in public as it violates the rights of the student and the coach. These are issues that belong in closed session under student discipline and personnel actions. The press and community cannot be briefed as it could violate due process. Such are the political realities of dealing with board policies concerning student and personnel discipline. The superintendent must judiciously navigate a fine line between protecting the student and coach while supporting board policy and managing the fallout from the situation. It requires administrative actions that are balanced and well-rooted in an ethical and practical belief system.

Take another situation that could easily happen to any district leader. The board is persuaded to take action due to bias against the superintendent voiced by a member(s) of the board, community, or the teachers union. Such politically motivated actions could lead to reprimand or even dismissal. Superintendents must be aware of the possibilities of such actions by boards. They should always have in place the protection of a legally binding written contract and personal conduct rooted in moral and ethical behavior supported by fair and equitable actions.

Consequences of board or superintendent actions based on bias or unsubstantiated personal allegations can lead to mistrust, anger, recriminations, and power struggles. Superintendents must remember they are agents of the board, but they must also balance this principle with a personal value and belief system that ultimately is supported by transparent actions, words, and deeds.

POLITICS, POLICIES, AND
MEETING THE NEEDS OF STUDENTS

It is not difficult to argue it is a priority that every child succeeds as ESSA suggests. The media continuously reports about the urgency associated with closing achievement gaps and in eliminating the education disparities between race and class so that all children can learn. Local school board elections are one place where citizens can make a difference, and where the dialogue can begin. Through technology, innovation, and strategic public involvement, we may move our schools to a more competitive advantage with other industrialized nations.

To create optimal conditions for student outcomes, local boards and superintendents must understand how their macro-level decisions impact principals, teachers, and students, and then align resources accordingly. Heavily influencing school districts are federal and state statutes and mandates that play a role in shaping local policy. For example, while curriculum decisions have historically been made at the local level, they are increasingly being influenced by state and federal policy as seen in the initiatives of the Common Core State Standards, the federal NCLB flexibility waivers, and ESSA, designed in large part to encourage and demand rigorous standards nationwide with improved student outcomes.

The literature examining the correlation between school board actions/ policies and student outcomes is limited and needs updating. Nevertheless, a seminal multiyear project entitled Lighthouse Study (2000), conducted by the Iowa Association of School Boards, documented a correlation between student achievement and the actions and beliefs of board members that has potential relevance. The original study and subsequent follow-up projects demonstrated that particular school board actions and beliefs transfer to district personnel and lead to better student outcomes even in high poverty districts. Specifically, the Lighthouse Study found the following board characteristics present in high-performing, high-poverty districts and missing in low-performing, high-poverty districts:

- Inspiring versus accepting belief systems (e.g., board members see schools as raising students' potential as opposed to seeing students' potential as fixed);
- Focusing on continuous school renewal and increased student performance (e.g., board members understand school improvement and change processes); and
- Action planning in schools and classrooms (e.g., board members are knowledgeable about school improvement plans [SIPs] and action planning processes).

The Lighthouse Study is important in school board research because it documents the correlation between school board attributes, actions, and student outcomes. A more recent study from the National School Boards Association (NSBA) focused on school board actions in developing diversity policies and the need to address learning for all students. This study actually followed up the NSBA's collaborative role in the Lighthouse Study. The NSBA study is titled, *Achieving Educational Excellence for All: A Guide to Diversity-Related Policy Strategies for School Districts* (2011).

This well-researched and reflective study states in the forward, "Our hope is that leaders at all levels of the school community, from school board members to educators, to superintendents and parents, use this resource to move the conversation forward about the importance of diversity as a means for achieving educational goals, and that they do so in a way that is not only legally sound, but also reflects the best values of the communities they serve" (NSBA, 2011, p. 5).

The study used recent research data and demographics to present a clear case that today is the time to meet the needs of our learners. The picture provided by this study of our national student population is a telling piece of data collection. Several highlights from the NSBA report (2011) reveal that:

- By 2050, racial and ethnic minority groups, who have the lowest rates of high school and college completion, will comprise 55 percent of the working-age population in America.
- Roughly two of every five black or Hispanic students attend segregated schools (in which 90 to 100 percent of students are minorities), up from less than one-third in 1988, while 8 percent of white students attend schools with 50 to 100 percent minority student populations.
- Segregation tends to be multidimensional with corresponding levels of socioeconomic and language isolation. More than 80 percent of segregated

black and Hispanic schools are poverty-concentrated, while only 5 percent of white schools are indicated as poverty-concentrated.

- Economically and racially isolated schools result in limited student access to opportunity networks for employment and postsecondary education. These schools generally provide fewer educational offerings and resources and have higher teacher turnover and lower teacher quality.
- Diverse schools produce educational and life-long benefits, enhancing civic values, improving student learning and preparation for employment, and increasing educational opportunities. Diverse schools provide students with deeper ways of thinking, higher aspirations, and positive interactions with students of other races and ethnicities. These are life experiences that translate into positive, long-term benefits for living and working in diverse settings (NSBA, 2011, p.11).

While school and district performance is influenced by complex internal and external factors, school board members are positioned to make a difference. Of note, the study points out that individual board members' belief systems shape their decisions and actions which influence the quality of schools. Furthermore, board members' level of knowledge of the schools and the initiatives designed to improve student learning can make a difference in outcomes. The challenge for board members is to obtain enough knowledge to make informed decisions, while guarding against using this knowledge to micromanage the superintendent and the district and school staffs.

As these examples make clear, a board and a superintendent's approach to policy development should not reflect a one-size-fits-all model, but one that includes specific educational goals and student needs, with consideration of community beliefs. Ultimately, policies should be framed around the unique educational needs of students. After all, the goal for every child to succeed should be achievable.

SUMMARY

This chapter reviewed the role of school boards and the superintendent in the public school educational process. School boards are one of the closest democratically elected entities to the community. They provide a wide array of services and assistance to the community. Citizens gain access to school district services and initiatives through board politics and practices. Yet, what becomes evident in communities across America is the impact that politics plays on the governance of local school districts.

The increasing role of the federal government was referenced in such federal laws as the Elementary and Secondary Education Act of 1965 (ESEA) amended in 2011, the Education for All Handicapped Children Act of 1975 (EHCA), the Individuals with Disabilities Education Act of 1997 (IDEA), the No Child Left Behind Act of 2001 (NCLB), and the Every Student Succeeds Act of 2015 (ESSA). Local control of education seems to erode with such initiatives as the Common Core State Standards. It appears more and more federal oversight is challenging boards and superintendents across the nation.

Studies were cited that shed light on the critical role boards have in establishment of policies in the public schools. Board policy development was highlighted to illustrate how boards can impact the day-to-day instruction of all learners. School boards must work with communities to support their diverse student populations and help create school cultures and climates in which student differences are acknowledged and celebrated.

There are conflicts within district and school settings that could occur between superintendents and boards of education. District and school leaders must create a balance between their own personal beliefs and values and those directed by the citizen-elected board of education. When conflict does occur, leaders need to rely on a strong ethical framework supported by a relevant conceptual framework of leadership theory.

CASE STUDY

You are a superintendent of a K–12 district with 6,000 students. Your homeless student procedures are guided by a board policy based on the federal McKinney-Vento Homeless Assistance Act. All students who are identified as homeless fall under specific guidelines as outlined in the district's homeless policy.

During the spring break, the district homeless liaison reports that a student has been reported as taking a bus every day from another community where he lives with his grandmother in an apartment. When the student enrolled, the grandmother claimed homelessness for the student. The recent report leads you to believe the student may be falsely enrolled and the grandmother may have made false claims to your district homeless liaison.

The student has been enrolled for one semester now and will return in a few days to finish the semester. What actions do you take to remedy the situation? How will you handle the student enrollment? Will you permit him to finish the semester to receive credit in his coursework or do you immediately drop him from attending school? What actions do you take concerning the grandparent? How will you involve legal counsel? What information should be shared with the board, the school faculty, the community, and the press?

EXERCISES AND DISCUSSION QUESTIONS

1. Research the McKinney-Vento Homeless Assistance Act and discuss how this federal law impacts the policies of a school district and the day-to-day operations of schools.
2. Research the policies of your school district concerning student attendance center assignment. Is your district policy fair and equitable for all students? What would you change or alter, if needed? Why? What is missing in the policy?
3. Research the student homeless policy of your district. Is your policy fair and do the steps outlined in the policy meet federal and state guidelines for homelessness? What would you change or alter, if needed? Why? What is missing in the policy?
4. Research your district board policy on ethics and conduct. Does the policy apply to board members as well as all school district employees? If not, what might the policy language contain? If yes, explain how it is fair and equitable to all parties involved.

REFERENCES

Alsbury, T. (Ed.). (2008). *The future of school board governance: Relevancy and revelation.* New York: Rowman & Littlefield Education.

Brown v. Board of Education, 347 U.S. 483 (1954).

Common Core State Standards Initiative. (2015). Retrieved from www.corestandards .org.

Education for All Handicapped Children Act of 1975. Public Law 94–142, 94th U.S. Congress. Retrieved from http://uscode.house.gov/statutes/pl/94/142.pdf.

Elementary and Secondary Education Amendments Act of 2011. S. 1571, 112th U.S. Congress. Retrieved from https://www.govtrack.us/congress/bills/112/s1571.

Every Student Succeeds Act (ESSA) of 2015. S. 1177, 114th U.S. Congress. Retrieved from https://www.congress.gov/bill/114th-congress/senate-bill/1177/text.

Iannaccone, L., & Lutz, F. W. (1970). *Politics, power, and policy: The governing of local school districts.* Columbus, OH: Charles E. Merrill Publishing.

Individuals with Disabilities Education Act Amendments of 1997. Public Law 105-17. Retrieved from https://www.naset.org/idea972.0.html#c9912.

IASB's Lighthouse Study. (2000, Fall). School boards and student achievement. Des Moines, IA: Iowa Association of School Boards, *Iowa School Board Compass, V*(2).

Lutz, F., & Iannaccone, L. (2008). The dissatisfaction theory of American democracy. In T. Alsbury (Ed.), *The future of school board governance: Relevancy and revelation*. New York: Rowman & Littlefield Education.

Moe, T. (2011). *Special interest: Teachers unions and America's public schools*. Washington DC: Brookings Institution Press.

National School Boards Association. (2011). *Achieving educational excellence for all: A guide to diversity-related policy strategies for school districts*. Alexandria, VA: Author.

No Child Left Behind Act of 2001. Public Law 107-110. Retrieved from http://www2.ed.gov/nclb/overview/intro/guide/guide_pg12.html#history.

Rada, R. D. (1987, April). An economic theory of school governance. Paper presented at the Annual Meeting of the American Educational Research Association, Washington, DC.

———. (1988). A public choice theory of school board member behavior. *Educational Evaluation and Policy Analysis 10*(3), 225–236.

U.S. Constitution, Amendment X (1791). Retrieved from http://www.senate.gov/civics/constitution_item/constitution.htm#amdt_10_(1791).

U.S. Department of Education, National Center for Education Statistics. (2013). *Digest of education statistics 2012* (NCES 2014–015), chapter 2.

Wirt, F. M., & Kirst, M. W. (1989). *Schools in conflict: The politics of education* (2nd ed.). Berkeley, CA: McCutchan Publishing Corp.

Zeigler, L. H., Jennings, M. K., & Peak, W. G. (1974). *Governing American schools: Political interaction in local school districts*. North Scituate, MA: Duxbury Press.

Chapter Five

Accountability and Professional Learning

The Superintendent as Supervisor and Evaluator

OBJECTIVES

At the conclusion of this chapter you will be able to:

1. Understand the importance of professional learning and growth as major influences in improving leader effectiveness (ELCC 1, 2, 3, 4, 5; PSEL 2, 4, 6, 7, 9, 10).
2. Describe the relationship between supervision and professional learning and growth in leadership development (ELCC 1, 2, 3; PSEL 2, 6, 7).
3. Describe the relationship between evaluation and professional learning and growth in leadership development (ELCC 1, 2, 3; PSEL 2, 6, 7).
4. Describe and use a suggested model for tracking professional learning and growth (ELCC 1, 2, 3, 4, 5, 6; PSEL 2, 6, 7).

PROFESSIONAL GROWTH

A superintendent must understand that the professional and personal needs of a novice school leader are far different than those of an experienced leader; however, we hold these leaders to the same expectations of competency and professionalism. The question becomes how to differentiate supervision and evaluation of these leaders, and how to help them grow in their leadership knowledge and skills. All leaders have different needs as they examine their own professional learning and growth.

Novice leaders need more intensive support and more frequent feedback to grow into highly effective practitioners than many district evaluation systems are designed to provide. The reality is that even the best prepared leaders need time and assistance to apply their knowledge and skills to their individual schools and districts. If supervision and evaluation are truly the focal point of a performance management and professional growth system, then they must be paired with structured support and ongoing, data-driven feedback that a comprehensive performance program should provide.

Too often professional development activities are structured as a one-size-fits-all. Most school districts only use a small portion of their budget for professional learning and growth activities for school or district leaders. Most often, there is no specific professional growth program planned for these leaders. They are usually combined with the same professional development given to the teaching or the support staff. And often, neither the leaders nor the support staff are even included in professional growth opportunities.

Those activities that leaders do attend may be relevant, but often overlook the requirements needed for effective leaders. It appears that school districts are not investing in the most important part of personnel management—that of ongoing, sustained learning and growth for those important leaders, a valued human resource supporting the district schools.

Yet professional growth and learning activities are used by leaders in planning continuous opportunities for teachers to grow in pedagogical techniques, knowledge, and content skills. This type of growth is often teacher-driven and geared directly to the individual needs of that teacher. These activities usually appear in the individual teacher supervision and evaluation plan.

But what about those activities needed for the leader to grow in leadership knowledge and skills? Where do these fit into an individual leader supervision and professional evaluation plan? This is where the superintendent can provide a climate and tools for dialogue, direction, and structure in a comprehensive and relevant professional growth plan for school and other district leaders.

As best-practice strategies for leadership continue to emerge in the literature, the standards-based movement and the licensing of educators have helped to develop recommendations for leadership preparation programs and the evaluation of leaders. Early in the history of leadership development, there were few suggested formal processes for evaluation of effective leadership.

Goal setting was based on simple tasks. Leaders were evaluated on the effectiveness of management skills such as orderly hallways, a clean school, providing adequate supplies for the classrooms and programs, and discipline handled with fair and efficient strategies. Yet in the past several decades, the functions required of leaders have now become much more complex. The literature calls for the leader to be an effective instructional leader with expert management and people skills, assessment knowledge, and skilled fiscal resource management.

SUPERVISION AND BUILDING CAPACITY FOR GROWTH

Educational research has repeatedly identified effective teaching and effective leadership as critical factors in student learning. The work that leaders accomplish in schools and classrooms matters and one of a district's top priorities should be to find, hire, and continuously develop leaders.

Supervision is formative. It provides coaching and mentoring to build leadership capacity and help guide novice and experienced leaders in searching out best research for sustained personal growth. Evaluation is summative. It is generally described as having two primary purposes: 1) measuring performance, and 2) providing individualized feedback and support to strengthen professional performance.

Many leadership supervision and evaluation procedures adopted by school districts do little to impact performance. Typically, leaders view the supervision and evaluation procedures as bureaucratic hurdles that must be cleared. They are simply one more task leaders must accomplish. This roadblock is magnified by the fact that many administrative supervision and evaluation plans do not require supervisors to visit schools or to review specific leadership actions in an ongoing manner to promote accountability and growth.

It is appropriate to have discussions about how to effectively supervise and evaluate leaders so the process is relevant to them and improves their leadership practice. Leadership supervision and evaluation must be guided by two major points: 1) effective school leadership is central to effective teacher supervision and evaluation, and 2) as teacher supervision and evaluation should be comprehensive in scope, so should leadership supervision and evaluation.

The district superintendency is essential to ensure that the supervision and evaluation of school and other district leaders is meaningful. Superintendents must adopt comprehensive and fair supervision and evaluation policies and practices. Most importantly, they must expect and hold school leaders accountable to be in teacher classrooms daily and weekly. This includes the central belief that district leaders are responsible for training and monitoring evaluators in how to ensure that teachers are providing high-quality instruction.

Effective supervisors routinely visit schools and provide formative, relevant, and appropriate feedback to leaders. Visiting schools on a routine basis is critical. How can we create a clear picture of leader effectiveness unless we formally and informally visit schools and classrooms multiple times per year? If we expect school leaders to be in all teacher classrooms weekly, for extended periods of time, then district leaders must hold them accountable for performing this task. If leadership development and personal growth is a priority, then superintendents must find ways to routinely visit schools and teacher classrooms. Districts must operationally define effective leadership and be clear about how to measure it.

The recent trend of using standardized or high-stakes state testing data as the standard for school effectiveness is flawed. Teaching is a social endeavor having many complex variables impacting student learning and leaders are significant in those variables. Student test scores should be used as one piece of data in a comprehensive leadership supervision and evaluation model. However, equally important are data collected from such varied sources as:

- classroom observations (assessed by principals, teacher leaders, instructional coaches, or peers),
- student assessment data on various indicators focused on growth (mostly formative assessments),
- instructional artifacts like student work, scoring rubrics, and lesson plans,
- teacher self-reflection within journals or logs,
- age-appropriate student or parent surveys,
- teacher-developed professional development/growth plans.

One key factor in selecting data sources is to ensure leaders have buy-in about what they perceive as fair and representative of their leadership performance. But superintendent supervisors should also have nonnegotiables in the process. These nonnegotiables may include such areas as:

- relevant and age-appropriate instructional schedules,
- clearly identified and posted essential learning standards in "student friendly" language,
- a school-wide behavior plan that supports and aligns with the district and school vision and mission,
- ongoing opportunities for students to achieve subject matter mastery.

There may be other nonnegotiables as determined by the school and district environment in which the leaders work. Supervisors must solicit feedback about leadership performance expectations throughout the supervisory process, if they expect the procedures to impact day-to-day school-wide classroom instructional practice.

When superintendents wear the supervisory hat, they are coaching, mentoring, collaborating, and actively assisting leaders in the school setting. They become another set of eyes and ears in the school and classrooms helping to improve and monitor student learning. The district leader creates opportunities for collaborative dialogue with the school leader to discuss classroom management systems, student behavior programs, instructional methodology, current research, and student learning goals.

The supervisory hat permits the district leader to be a mentor and to guide the school leader to relevant and effective research in best practices. Together the district leader and school leader can develop relevant goals for growth that directly impact the day-to-day learning of students, teachers, and support staff. Figure 5.1 provides the elements of an effective and ongoing supervisory plan.

Generally speaking, all leaders can benefit from good coaching and mentoring. Mentoring can help leaders when faced with issues in dealing with disruptive students, personal problems that impact teaching, administrative requirements, state and district reporting, and clarifying the responsibilities of the position. District leaders should be well trained in how to be effective supervisors in the mentoring and coaching process.

In supervision, the relationship between supervisor and school leader is critical to success in personal and professional growth. Topics for coaching and mentoring may include understanding instruction and curriculum, managing student discipline, understanding the school district operations, and district policies and procedures. In addition to these professional qualities, a mentor needs effective coaching skills which include being personal, sensitive, understanding, establishing rapport, and giving constructive feedback (Tomal et al., 2014).

Finally, it should be noted that the summative evaluation process is simply an analysis of data collected during the supervision process. Sustained supervision is the only way to improve leadership practice. Resources need to be

Effective Supervision

- Requires ongoing coaching and mentoring
- Promotes sharing of collaborative ideas
- Provides constructive feedback
- Has multiple informal and formal building visits
- Provides effective counseling and monitoring
- Includes conflict mediation when needed
- Requires measureable and relevant goals
- Focuses on realistic outcomes

Figure 5.1. Qualities of an effective leadership supervision plan.

devoted to the improvement of these practices rather than simply assigning a rating to performance. What then is the necessary role of evaluation in the supervision and evaluation process?

EVALUATION AND BUILDING CAPACITY FOR GROWTH

Like students, leaders also are learners. The best way to improve student learning is to strengthen the instructional practices of leaders through job-embedded professional learning opportunities. Evaluation systems have a critical role to play in informing this work, and the ones conceived with this in mind will be most likely to succeed.

Leadership evaluation must focus more on the act of being a leader. Policies and procedures must not only measure performance, but also provide pathways to develop and improve practice. A well-designed evaluation plan might better be termed a performance management plan. Its primary purposes must be to maximize the act of leadership and to improve performance. It does so as a critical component of an aligned district-wide process which provides embedded opportunities for leaders to continuously learn and grow.

Evaluation is most effective when it is integrated with other processes that support professional learning and growth. It needs to provide individual leaders with the opportunity 1) to analyze the process, 2) to determine the impact on their individual roles, and 3) to make modifications based on that analysis. What leaders need is fewer performance ratings and more data-driven feedback on their practice. A commitment to ongoing leader learning, including the creation of personalized professional learning plans, should be a central focus in a comprehensive evaluation process.

These plans should point leaders toward specific and highly relevant learning opportunities that allow them to address areas of leadership that need improvement. It means that evaluators must understand effective leadership. This will only happen when those responsible for evaluating, coaching, and mentoring leaders are trained in the art of providing meaningful, developmental feedback, encouraging reflection, and creating opportunities for professional learning and growth.

If designed as part of a comprehensive plan, feedback on instruction, reflection, and mentoring activities changes professional development from a one-time or infrequent event to continuous growth activities. It is critical that districts build these principles and structures into their evaluation processes because a systemic evaluation plan will succeed or fail based on its ability to improve leadership capacity, instructional pedagogy, and ultimately student learning.

Figure 5.2 provides the qualities of an effective evaluation process.

The models or frameworks used for evaluation of leaders must be research-based. What is important is that the evaluators and the leaders 1) need to agree upon the model and the process that will be used, 2) have a shared language, and 3) have a common understanding and definition of the elements of effective leadership.

A meaningful evaluation process transitions directly from a relevant supervisory process. An honest evaluation with reliable and constructive feedback based on evidence without bias will enable leaders to continue to learn and grow. Both are based on developing a collaborative and trusting coaching/mentoring relationship between the leader and the evaluator.

When superintendents wear the evaluator's hat, they gather evidence and data from multiple sources and make judgments about performance. These sources may include student surveys, classroom observations, classroom drop-ins, and student achievement results gleaned from standardized summative and formative district and grade-level assessments. All of the data gathered must be analyzed by leaders and the evaluator to identify professional growth needs. One comprehensive way to conduct this analysis is through standards-based leadership models, such as PSEL or ELCC. Such elements of leadership tasks and competencies as seen in these standards can help to successfully measure leadership effectiveness and provide leaders with relevant feedback on the factors that matter for improving performance and enhancing professional growth.

Effective Evaluation

- Is research and outcome based
- Has developmental and meaningful feedback
- Includes measureable goals
- Has active and ongoing reflection
- Provides opportunities for continuing growth
- Builds leadership knowledge
- Builds leadership capacity
- Impacts teacher and student performance
- Provides a rating of performance

Figure 5.2. Qualities of an effective leadership evaluation plan.

School districts can create alignment between evaluator priorities and coaching priorities by using standards-based models to guide individual leader evaluation, self-assessment, and mentoring. This necessitates a system of open communication and trust between leaders and evaluators. It requires a shared protocol (common language) for assessing leadership and a genuine understanding of the culture and climate of the district and schools.

RESEARCH-BASED SUPERVISION AND EVALUATION

By enhancing and building upon a modified clinical supervision model, we can use it as a tool for change and growth that results in more effective leadership and increased individual growth. The traditional administrative evaluation process has usually been a one-way progression. This process has typically consisted of the following steps:

1. Written notification of a conference—Leader receives a fall notice that an evaluation is due usually in the spring of the school year. The leader is invited to a conference with the superintendent or a designee to discuss goals and strategies for that school year.
2. Conference—Conversation with leader regarding submission of goals, updates, and key dates for submission of information to evaluator. Brief discussions about management, budgeting, and personnel usually dominate the conference.
3. Follow-up conference—Administrator shows up at appointed time and submits a summative narrative of the actions and results from the goal conference earlier in the school year.
4. Narrative write up—Evaluator fills out required district forms for administrative evaluation and provides copies for the administrator by the required approved timeline (which either conforms to state statutes and/or Board administrative policy and procedures).
5. Post-narrative conference—Leader and evaluator discuss written evaluation and performance rating. Both leader and evaluator sign off as having read and discussed the written document regarding the evaluation process.
6. Sign off with signatures—Both parties agree that they have concluded the process required.

Unfortunately, on-site observations rarely or never occur in this model. The effectiveness of the leader may not be representative of what students, teachers, and parents experience on a daily basis.

Often in school districts, there is a lack of alignment between observation and gathering hard data as evidence. There is little or no planning for professional learning and growth for the leader in the evaluation cycle. Basically, the traditional evaluation process is a time-intensive process without much impact on leader effectiveness or teacher-student performance. Leaders become passive recipients in the evaluation process isolated from their peers. For leaders to professionally grow in an effective evaluation process, they must be active and reflective participants.

When a research-based model is implemented, a training period is needed for both evaluators and leaders. They must become familiar with the steps in the supervisory and evaluation process. They must share knowledge and develop a common language defining effective teaching. They must develop a shared understanding of what constitutes effective instruction and the expectations of leaders in that district to meet those expectations.

It is possible that leaders who in the past have received high performance ratings may now receive lower ratings. This may create an uncomfortable climate for some leaders, who may have received high ratings using a traditional supervision and evaluation model based on written narratives every year. In the worst-case scenario, there is no written feedback for the leader and there is no performance evaluation on a yearly basis.

Superintendents need to develop strategies for supporting and improving school leaders throughout the evaluation process. Expectations must be raised. Resources and key learning opportunities are vital to improving leadership performance when using a research-based evaluation plan. What is important to the evaluation and supervision of leaders is the central premise that leaders must grow in expertise to become more effective in their demanding and complex roles.

The effective superintendent should establish clear and fair guidelines for the evaluation and supervisory process. These may include:

- the use of a collaborative goal-setting process,
- the establishment of mutually agreed-upon nonnegotiables for student achievement and assessment,
- a clear alignment to school improvement plans and the values, vision, mission, and goals of the district and the school,
- a research-based data collection process that monitors and documents ongoing achievement and instructional goals,
- the allocation of resources to support the goals for achievement and instruction in the school and district.

All of these actions must be implemented collaboratively when working with individual leaders. Guiding this process must be a clear vision and mission for the district and schools supporting the principle that every child can learn. Student performance goals should permit students multiple opportunities to demonstrate what they have learned and show that they can use the knowledge and skills identified within the established district curriculum. Creative leadership is central to supporting a systemic use of the professional learning and growth supervisory evaluation process.

INDIVIDUAL PROFESSIONAL LEARNING AND GROWTH PLANS

The use of a modified supervision and evaluation model, which reflects the ELCC and the PSEL standards, may be one step to beginning an effective supervision and evaluation plan for leaders. These standards explicitly demonstrate that the purpose of professional learning is for educators to develop the knowledge, skills, practices, and dispositions they need to help students perform at higher levels. The standards are not a prescription for how education leaders and public officials should address all the challenges related to improving the performance of educators and their students. Instead, they focus on the central issue of professional traits and competencies evident in successful and effective leaders.

So, if a superintendent evaluator creates the environment for effective evaluation, the dialogue between the evaluator and leader would include a discussion of those elements written into job descriptions combined with what constitutes effective leadership as demonstrated in the national standards like ELCC and PSEL. These then become the foundation on which to build the supervisory and evaluation process.

To develop a new perspective for leader-focused professional learning and growth, there is a need to create a learning organization with identified leadership learning communities committed to continuous improvement, collective accountability, and goal alignment. Allotting time and resources for collaboration by this leadership community on a regular basis during the school day, months, and year is a requirement.

In addition, training in teaming skills will assist with the transformation of the culture and climate of the individual, the group, and the organization. If smaller districts cannot accommodate this type of learning community within the district, then combining with surrounding smaller districts into a larger, more relevant leadership community may be necessary. The point is leaders need support and that is best done in collaboration with others in the same or similar roles.

Supervisors and evaluators must also act as instructional leaders. They must articulate the overall vision and mission of the district. The overarching principle is that all students must have the opportunity to master the knowledge and skills identified in an articulated curriculum aligned with national and state standards. Finally, there is a fundamental need for leaders, teachers, and students to be life-long learners with continuous individual, group, and organizational improvement as the underlying foundation of the district as a learning community.

Even though each leader is looked upon as a life-long learner in a professional learning community, it is important to differentiate the need for and the quantity of supervision and evaluation of the leaders. Leaders who receive performance ratings such as distinguished, exceeding, or excellent, depending on the rating scale used, may not need to be evaluated every year. Leaders who receive performance ratings such as proficient or satisfactory may need to be evaluated every other year and encouraged to continue to grow so that they enhance their personal and professional growth.

However, novice leaders who need much coaching and mentoring, and those experienced leaders who receive ratings such as basic, unsatisfactory, or needs improvement must be monitored more closely on an annual basis. If their status remains unchanged, consideration should be given to dismissal as they may not have the ability to grow or improve or they are choosing not to grow professionally. Addressing the unsatisfactory and marginal leader is necessary in an effective district supervisory and evaluation plan. Schools cannot continue to grow and function with ineffective and poorly functioning leadership. These are the schools that consistently become labeled for watch lists or in need of improvement. Most importantly, the performance level of the children in these schools is compromised and learning may be delayed.

When leaders are ineffective in schools, they impact student performance in a profoundly negative way. It is unfair to the students attending an ineffective or marginal school, as they may not have the same opportunities to perform as their peers who have been enrolled in a more effective school. Field research has clearly documented that effective classroom practices in higher-performing schools result in higher-achieving learners.

Mid-Continent Research for Education and Learning (McREL) conducted a study in 2001 about what works in schools in a large-scale, systematic way. This meta-analysis reviewed decades of studies focused on teacher classroom practice. They then selected the most rigorous from an initial sampling of 4,000 such studies. McREL's researchers mathematically determined the most effective practices found to have a statistically significant impact on student learning measured by standardized test scores.

First published in 2001, this study described in *Classroom Instruction That Works* (Marzano et al., 2001) changed teaching by linking classroom strategies to evidence of increased student learning. The work clearly identified successful approaches that mark effective classroom instruction. The basic premise of the study was to show that schools that use research to guide instructional practices out-perform those that do not.

In a companion book, *What Works in Schools*, Marzano (2003) describes eleven research-based factors shown in another large-scale research project at McREL to be essential for the larger context of an effective school. The study was a follow-up of that done in 2001 and verified once again that teacher effectiveness is of high importance. The study was categorized into three areas of school, teacher, and student factors.

The school factors were a guaranteed and viable curriculum, challenging goals and effective feedback, parent and community involvement, a safe and orderly environment, and collegiality and professionalism. The teacher factors were instructional strategies, classroom management, and effective curriculum design. The student factors were home environment, learned intelligence and background knowledge, and motivation. These eleven factors led to the conclusion that school effectiveness and teacher effectiveness are highly interrelated in how a student learns (Marzano, 2003).

In his 90-90-90 studies, Reeves (2005) showed that high-poverty schools could also be high-performing. He provided examples from multiple school systems to illustrate the common characteristics of 90/90/90 schools (over 90 percent poverty, over 90 percent minorities, and yet over 90 percent achieving at high proficiency levels). The factors identified in the studies were: a strong focus on academic achievement, clear curriculum choices, frequent assessment of student progress and multiple opportunities for improvement, an emphasis on nonfiction writing, and collaborative scoring of student work, with explicit guidelines.

Reeves stressed that teacher quality and effective leadership, not demographics, are the most dominant factors in determining student success. The effective practices and policies identified in those studies are entirely consistent with the McREL's findings. It is these types of studies that effective leaders can use to improve the teaching and learning in schools and to guide ongoing and effective professional learning opportunities. That is why relevant professional learning and the tracking of individual teacher growth are vital to creating effective teachers.

It is also why professional and learning growth plans are essential for effective leaders who evaluate and supervise teachers. That is one of the reasons why evaluators of leaders need to have the moral courage to deal with unsatisfactory and marginal leaders. It is an unpleasant task. It is an ethical task that needs to be carried through if we are following a vision of a learning organization with all members being life-long learners. True instructional leaders will ensure that every child is receiving an equal opportunity to learn with an effective teacher and an equally effective leader.

In this environment, leaders will be expected to continue to learn, to improve, and to become more effective in their roles. The expectations are set by the norms of the learning organization and its collective members. This will have a profound impact on the entire district and schools as each leader becomes more effective no matter their performance level. It is possible that the whole professional learning organization will collectively and individually demonstrate improvement. This improvement will positively impact the learning goals and performance levels of the students served by the organization.

In the research-based environment, accountability and more supervisory hands-on guidance and coaching are required. As an instructional leader, the superintendent and other district leaders are out in classrooms observing and studying what works in the schools. In addition, effective district and school leaders will use the talent and expertise of identified effective teacher leaders to coach and mentor those peers who are given a rating of "unsatisfactory" or "needs improvement" to help improve teacher effectiveness.

Superintendents who are planning for school leader growth must develop capacity, must advocate, and must create support systems for professional learning. They must prioritize, monitor, and coordinate resources and make them available for each leader no matter the level of experience. Multiple forms and sources of data should be used to identify individual needs as the evaluator plans, assesses, and evaluates professional leadership knowledge, skills, and traits (see figure 5.3).

- Has active leader and supervisor collaboration
- Is research and evidence based
- Has measureable goals
- Contains a mutually agreed upon action plan
- Includes a manageable timeline
- Contains mutually agreed upon resources
- Has realistic and measurable evidence
- Builds leadership capacity
- Includes best instructional strategies and practices
- Impacts classroom instruction
- Improves leader, teacher, and student performance

Figure 5.3.   Elements of a leadership professional learning and growth plan.

Using this model for professional learning and growth, an effective and comprehensive goal-setting evaluation process can be developed. In appendix B, there are several sample plans for professional learning and growth. The plans are outlined for easy understanding following the elements outlined in figure 5.3. Each sample plan can be aligned to such standards as ELCC, PSEL, even the AASA, Professional Standards for the Superintendency with each component aligned to a goal or goals set by the leader. The evaluator and the leader being evaluated could prepare two to three goals aligned to the standards for the performance supervision and evaluation process.

Each goal has an established timeline, person responsible, action steps, and evidence of what was accomplished within the time frame established. Using such a tool for the supervision and evaluation of a school or district leader allows for the fair and transparent process of performance rating and, more importantly, sustained professional growth that is controlled by the leader while benefiting the school and district stakeholders.

The application of a research-based approach to supervision and evaluation should be applied with sustained support during implementation until long-term change is embedded in the culture of the organization. The evaluation process should be an outgrowth of the supervisory process. The outcomes should align with national and state standards, content standards, district vision and mission, school improvement plans, and most importantly, the expected learning goals of the district. The ultimate goals must always be improved student performance paired with leader and teacher continuing professional growth.

SUMMARY

An analysis of research data has indicated that effective leadership is one of the most important variables directly impacting student performance. All children deserve to have an effective leader in their school. Research and field practice have defined what elements comprise relevant and effective professional development plans. Such district and school plans must contain multiple learning and growth opportunities. These activities must target individual professional learning and growth based on the needs of the leader and the level of experience and background they have had in a leadership role.

How do we support and encourage leaders to become more effective in what they do? An answer is in a research-based and comprehensive evaluation and supervision plan focused on individual needs. This requires that superintendents act as effective evaluators and supervisors. They must be in schools and classrooms on a regular basis, provide immediate and reliable feedback about what was observed, and provide constructive suggestions for growth to the school leader.

At the same time, an improved formal evaluation process must emerge that will require school and district leaders to use information gathered from multiple sources, such as walk-throughs, student surveys, and other methods of gathering data over time. This enhanced process allows the evaluator to become more informed about the leader's performance, the climate and the culture of the school, and the classrooms. Effective supervision and evaluation must reflect a true picture of the daily life of a leader, the students, and the teachers in that school.

Using all of the data collected, the superintendent and school leader can identify professional needs and develop an individual professional learning and growth plan with goals, action steps, timeline, person responsible, resources, and evidence of completion. All leaders will have a professional learning and growth plan. Everyone will be considered a life-long learner and an active participant in the professional learning community with a goal of becoming a more effective and skilled leader.

CASE STUDY

You have been appointed as the new superintendent of two rural school districts. One district has a student enrollment of 150 and the other has an enrollment of 270. These two rural district boards of education have gone into partnership to hire you. They want to enhance the professionalism of the staff and provide instructional growth for the students of their districts. Therefore, they have decided to jointly hire you. The smaller district has one building and one experienced principal of five years. The other district has two schools with newly hired principals. Both districts feed to a consolidated county high school. In your induction with the boards, supervision and evaluation of faculty and the principals was extensively discussed. The boards asked that you develop professional learning and growth plans to be added to the supervision and evaluation process, which includes final performance ratings of Excellent, Proficient, Basic, and Unsatisfactory.

You have scheduled a conference with your three principals to jointly decide the focus for your first year as superintendent. Think about what you will suggest to your principals about their professional and personal growth. What areas do you wish to focus on in your first year? What types of support do you think they will need? You have decided to use the PSEL, 2015 leadership standards as a basic foundation for the learning and growth plans.

EXERCISES AND DISCUSSION QUESTIONS

1. What leadership elements of PSEL will you focus your attention on in your first year?
2. What will the professional learning plans list as possible activities for consideration as evidence of performance?
3. What steps will you take to collect appropriate data to support your actions?
4. What evidence will you determine is needed so that a fair and accurate appraisal is given about performance?
5. What steps will you take to establish a positive relationship with your principals and teaching staff?
6. What is the difference between evaluation and supervision? Can an evaluator wear both hats at the same time? If so, how?
7. Why is it important for a district to select a framework for supervision and evaluation that can be used by all leaders? How does this framework help leaders to become more effective?

Self-Assessment and Reflection

Develop a professional learning and growth plan for yourself based on your identified needs and professional goals. Develop a plan that includes the following: measureable goals, action steps, timeline, resources, person responsible, evidence submitted, and what impact and application it has to your role as a superintendent. What kind of professional development do you think you need? What role does the board play in your professional learning and growth plan?

REFERENCES

Marzano, R. (2003). *What works in schools: Translating research into action.* Alexandria, VA: ASCD.

Marzano, R., Pickering, D., & Pollock, J. (2001). *Classroom instruction that works: Research-based strategies for increasing student achievement.* Alexandria, VA: ASCD.

Reeves, D. (2005). *Accountability in action: A blueprint for learning organizations.* (2nd ed.). Denver: Advanced Learning Press.

Tomal, D., Schilling, C., & Wilhite, R. (2014). *The teacher leader: Core competencies and strategies for effective leadership.* Lanham, MD: Rowman & Littlefield.

Tomal, D., Wilhite, R., Phillips, B., Sims, P., & Gibson, N. (2015). *Supervision and evaluation for learning and growth.* Lanham, MD: Rowman & Littlefield.

Chapter Six

Follow Me, I Know the Way

Building District Capacity for Success

OBJECTIVES

At the conclusion of this chapter you will be able to:

1. Understand the district administration planning process (ELCC 1, 3; PSEL 1, 6, 10).
2. Define the steps of strategic and succession planning (ELCC 1, 3; PSEL 1, 6, 10).
3. Understand critical team values necessary to collaboratively develop a vision and effectively manage the district administration team (ELCC 1, 2, 3, 5; PSEL 1, 6, 7, 10).
4. Design a professional development plan for the administrative team (ELCC 1, 2, 3, 5; PSEL 6, 7, 10).

STRATEGIC PLANNING

So, how does a superintendent start to move forward and build capacity for the advancement of the school district? Where does one begin? What major actionable items contribute to all of this? One of the best places to start is to ensure that there is a good district management team in place, and that there are clear and meaningful school-wide district goals and a strategic plan that can guide the entire district to success. And, while there are many facets to leading a school district, the foundation begins with proper planning.

School district strategic planning ensures that an organization has the correct number of people in the right places at the right time who have the necessary skills to fulfill the vision of the institution. An organization cannot accomplish any meaningful goals without a well-qualified and functioning district administrative team.

Proper planning allows the superintendent to ensure that the administrative team is fully capable of leading everyone in the organization in accomplishing the tasks of the strategic plan and guiding the school district to success. While school district leaders may approach strategic planning differently, all members on the team need to be involved in the process. There also need to be capable people championing the initiatives throughout the organization.

Strategic planning is one of the most popular strategies utilized by school district leaders to prepare a comprehensive school district plan for meeting the needs of the future. Essentially, strategic planning involves answering the questions of "What is our situation today?" "Where do we want to go?" "How can we best get there?" and "Who are the people who are going to champion the strategies in getting us there?"

Strategic planning is a technique that originated in corporate America and has become a popular tool in education. This process allows administrators to identify critical issues to be addressed, establish an overall vision, and develop major goals, key strategies, metrics (commonly called key performance indicators), and resources needed to accomplish the goals.

While strategic planning has many benefits, it needs to be undertaken in a structured manner. If managed poorly, the costs of strategic planning can exceed the benefits. Individuals may waste valuable time in brainstorming ideas that are unproductive if the process is not well facilitated. Some limitations include: spending too much time on immediate needs without regard for long-term needs, failing to successfully implement strategies, lacking accountability, and failing to assess the progress of the strategic plan (Connerly, 2104).

Therefore, when strategic planning is undertaken, agreed-upon expectations are needed to ensure success. Some of these include providing sufficient time to develop the strategic plan, allowing for creativity, selecting the proper people who will participate and develop the plan, and providing sufficient financial resources to implement the strategic plan.

The procedure for conducting strategic planning can vary from organization to organization. Typically, strategic planning should begin at the top level with the superintendent and then be facilitated throughout the entire organization. For example, strategic planning could start at the district level with the superintendent and administrative team, be conducted at the school building level, and then at the department level. In this way all organizational units are supporting the top district-level initiatives, and the process is collaborative (Cal State LA, 2016).

The process of conducting strategic planning involves several critical steps (see figure 6.1). The first step is to assemble the strategic planning

Figure 6.1. Steps in conducting a strategic plan.

team. Typically, this team will consist of the superintendent and his or her administrative team and perhaps selected teachers and staff members. This team will not only be responsible for developing the final product, but will be responsible in driving the process and determining the resources needed for completing the strategic plan. Typically, this team will meet to plan all the resources needed and decide whether an outside facilitator should be used for the process.

The use of an outside facilitator can be helpful in allowing the entire team to concentrate on the content of the plan rather than needing to facilitate and record all the information which can be done by the facilitator. The facilitator can also conduct the process, reduce pressure from superiors, and help keep the group on track. While there is often a cost in utilizing outside facilitators, they can be valuable in providing input especially if they have past experience in conducting strategic planning with other organizations. They can also be helpful to the team when the members encounter difficult interpersonal and process issues.

The strategic plan is a road map for the organization and should include specific initiatives that support student learning. The strategic plan should also be a comprehensive document that includes plans for departments of the organization such as building facilities, human resources, engineering, technology, business finance, and academic and support service departments.

The school improvement plan (SIP) is similar to the strategic plan but it generally centers more on student learning such as curriculum and instruction, student and faculty programs, and student behavior that impacts the school. Therefore, the strategic plan is the overall road map that may include the SIP or support it.

The first step also consists of selecting the format for the strategic plan document. There are many variations in the components of a strategic plan. For example, some school districts may not have both a vision and mission statement. Also, depending upon the complexity of a school district, the number of departmental or unit plans can vary. Figure 6.2 shows an example of the typical components of a strategic plan.

It is important that the team determine the logistics in completing the strategic plan such as how often they will meet, location, schedule, materials, and other resources. Some teams may schedule multiple sessions which range from two-to-four hours over an extended period of time such as four-to-six

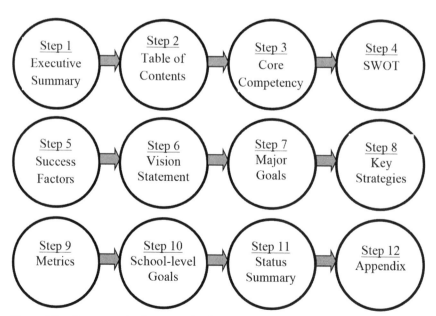

Figure 6.2. Components of a strategic plan.

weeks. However, sometimes the strategic planning team may conduct a special retreat where they may spend one or two concentrated days developing the plan. Each team must decide the overall logistics that are best for them and least obtrusive to the operation of the school.

Step two involves the team constructing a values statement. It is important to establish the key values that drive the behavior of people within the organization. Establishing values often is a prerequisite to writing a vision statement. For example, if the institution is a religious-based organization, the values will be different than for a public institution. Establishing these values can help in crafting the ultimate vision and mission statements.

When examining the values, some of the questions that can help guide the team include: "What values are important to us?" "What do we stand for?" "What specific behaviors do we embrace?" "How do we desire to treat each other?" and "How do we want to be viewed by our stakeholders?" Typically, by answering these questions a team will arrive at a values statement. In addition, team members can participate in values exercises to establish common team values for the group.

Figure 6.3 shows a list of typical values that team members could review and rank in order of importance for their team's success in working together in a group. For example, in this exercise the team members might determine that a value of individual power can be destructive to the overall cohesiveness of the team. In other words, the team members may decide that seeking individual power should be restrained while other values such as honesty and trust should be encouraged and reinforced for achieving team success.

Writing the vision statement, step three, typically includes thoughtful reflection about the desired outcome of the organization. Some helpful questions consist of "How do we achieve the highest quality learning within the school district?" "How can we support a culture that strives to treat people with honesty, respect, and open communications?" "How can we provide an opportunity for everyone to achieve?" and "How do we produce an organization of innovation, originality, and intellectual curiosity?"

Some teams may elect to write a mission statement in addition to a vision statement. Either a vision statement or a mission statement, or both, can be written. A mission statement tends to be a broad outcome such as "To explore the galaxies." A vision statement is typically much more concrete such as "To land a man on the moon and watch him walk." While the statements are similar, the vision statement concentrates more on behaviors and is often more tangible and measurable.

For example, a school district may have a mission statement "To allow all students to grow to their fullest capacity," versus a vision statement such as "All students will score in the top 20 percent of the nation on standardized

Figure 6.3.   Typical values of a school district leadership team.

tests." However, organizations are unique organisms and need to determine what kind of vision and mission statements best reflect the desires of the stakeholders. Also, perhaps a school district might include only one or the other to avoid confusion.

Step four consists of completing the SWOT analysis. SWOT stands for strengths, weaknesses, opportunities, and threats. In this step, the team identifies the strengths of the school district. Examples include a good core reputation, strong leadership, competent and experienced teachers, and high employee morale and satisfaction.

Weaknesses might include lack of technology equipment and expertise, inadequate safety, security, and transportation for students. Opportunities are those items that offer potential additional support to the school district in achieving higher performance levels such as: establishing community relationships, utilizing university expertise, writing grants, and increasing financial resources.

Threats are typically factors that might hinder the success of the school district. Examples include: an aging faculty, high employee attrition, political unrest within the community, and potential high immigrant growth that may require additional programs and resources. Establishing the strengths, weaknesses, opportunities, and threats can become the basis from which the strategic plan is developed. Often, the strengths are recognized and sometimes improved but the weaknesses need to be addressed by establishing concrete goals and key strategies. In addition, opportunities and threats need to be examined and strategic goals written to address them.

Step five entails writing the major goals for the strategic plan. These major goals should be written using SMART criteria. SMART goals consist of being specific, measurable, attainable, realistic, and timely. Once the major goals are written, it is important to carefully examine the goals and prioritize them. Remember, a team may write too many goals that cannot be realistically achieved. The team members should decide which are the highest priority goals and establish time frames for each of the goals such as one- to three-year increments. The dynamics of a school district change so it is necessary to review and revise them each year.

School districts often have four to seven major goals. Examples of these goal areas (or themes) include:

- Curriculum, Instruction, Quality, and Assessment
- Teacher and Leader Effectiveness
- Community Involvement and Communications
- School Culture and Student-Centered Support
- Financial, Resources, Safety, and Technology Sustainability
- Student Achievement and Accountability

Prioritizing the major goals and establishing time frames involves negotiation, collaboration, and resource management. Team members need to be respectful of each other and establish ground rules in how they conduct themselves in the meetings. Typical functional behaviors include seeking and giving opinions, elaborating and encouraging people to praise others, and being open to new ideas. Nonfunctional behaviors are being too aggressive, self-confessing, playing politics, pushing self-interest, withdrawal, clowning around, and disrupting the group.

Once the major goals are written, key strategies must be developed, step six. For example, if someone wants to become a millionaire, the key strategy outlines the process in "how to get the money?" If a major school district goal is to advance the knowledge and technical skills of the faculty, then one key strategy might be to hire a technology consultant and to conduct technology training sessions.

The use of metrics, sometimes called key performance indicators (KPIs), are the scorecards upon which the level of performance is to be established.

For example, if the school district's major goal is to improve technology knowledge and the key strategy is to provide training for people, a metric might be to achieve 50 percent competency within three months.

Step seven requires the development of the final strategic plan, which also includes disseminating the document to all stakeholders. The writing of the strategic plan requires careful review and editing by the members of the team to produce a high-quality document. Outside readers can be obtained to help critique the final document and ensure high acceptable quality and standards that are in line with any federal and state policies and guidelines. The final strategic plan is often approved by the strategic planning team, superintendent, or school board.

This step may also include integrating the strategic plan into the performance management system. This entails selecting the key goals and responsible people and holding them accountable through the performance appraisal process. This step is often overlooked in the strategic planning process. It is important that there is linkage between the goals and individuals' performance so people can be evaluated based upon the results. In some organizations, actual bonuses are given to individuals who exceed the goals which provide incentives for meeting and exceeding the goals.

Assigning champions for the major goals may be included in this step. Champions can act as crusaders in promoting the goals, providing resources needed to accomplish the goals, and measuring the results. They should be selected based upon the criteria of high credibility and strong desire for achieving results. They also should be people who have good interpersonal skills and who can work collaboratively with people to support actions in accomplishing the goals.

This step should also include disseminating the strategic plan to all stakeholders so they are aware of the plan. The strategic plan is not going to be accepted or worthwhile if it is locked up in a cabinet and no one knows about it. It is a living document that should be integrated within the entire school district and everyone should become involved in achieving it. Therefore, conducting awareness sessions for everyone within the organization can be a helpful way to explain the plan and to let people know how they can be involved in achieving the goals of the plan.

The success of any strategic plan can never be achieved without proper monitoring and assessing its progress, step eight. Therefore, a process for evaluating the school district's goals should be established which might consist of periodic review meetings and conducting district-wide update sessions with everyone.

This step may also include performance reviews of the individuals who are responsible for achieving the major goals. This can be done through the

Major Goals and Key Strategies with Metrics	Responsible People	Target Dates	Status
Major Goal 1: To obtain 100% integration of technology into instruction. Key Strategy #1: To conduct professional development technology programs for all teachers and achieve 100% competency in the technology development programs.	Assistant Superintendent for Curriculum and Instruction	Date	First program of three conducted on schedule and all teachers completed the program with 100% competency.

Figure 6.4. Example of a strategic planning spreadsheet.

performance appraisal process and periodic review meetings. Lastly, this step can also include an evaluation of the strategic planning process through extensive follow-up sessions by the original strategic plan members.

The evaluation might consist of what things went well, those things that did not go well, and ideas for improving the process the next time. Also, in monitoring the goals of a strategic plan it can be helpful to develop a spreadsheet listing each of the major goals, the key strategies and metric for each goal, who is responsible, target completion dates, and status. In this way the goals can easily be reviewed and comments can be written in the status section on the progress on each of the goals (see figure 6.4).

SUCCESSION PLANNING

Succession planning is a common practice in identifying and securing internal and external people to fill key administrative leadership positions within the organization to ensure sufficient human resource capacity. This process can be one of the most valuable ways to ensure that human resource needs are met. Generally, succession planning, or sometimes called replacement planning, is used for identifying successors for all administrative and staff positions.

Oliver Wendell Holmes once stated that, "The great thing in this world is not so much where we stand as in what direction we are going." The whole essence of succession planning is to be able to look into the future and ascertain which key positions need to be replaced. The succession planning process ensures that there is a successful transition of a candidate for a key position for the eventual retirement or unexpected separation of the incumbent from the position.

More simply stated, having a viable succession plan in place in the event of an abrupt departure of a key person can help weather the transition period, maintain operational continuity, and ensure the successful selection of a replacement in a timely manner. Generally, it is important that the superintendent establish a succession plan working with the school board. There needs to be a culture of honesty, trust, and mutual respect among members because inherent conflicts and misunderstanding are natural during this process. Therefore, the necessity of self-examination, critical analysis of current performance, spirited discussions, and candidness are hallmarks in balancing the multiplicity of viewpoints (Larcker & Saslow, 2014).

The succession plan should be an ongoing and dynamic process that is regularly updated. It isn't something that should be viewed as a one-time exercise. The process can also serve as a useful process for self-examination, assessment of organizational current and future needs, and continuous improvement.

The succession planning process often begins by identifying possible candidates for selected positions to be filled.

It is important to determine the future needs of the organization versus focusing on past needs. School district leaders who work collectively with an incumbent are more likely to establish a successful plan that is right for the future needs of the organization. In other words, if a key person is replaced, the dynamics of the administrative team may be impacted due to the varying skill sets that all the team members and the incumbent have. Some typical questions for thoughtful reflection include:

- Is there an up-to-date job description and set of core competencies for the position?
- What are mutual expectations of the school board and school district leadership team?
- What are the major responsibilities for an ideal person in this position? (versus the current job responsibilities of the position which might have evolved based upon the skills and talents of the incumbent, existing administrative team members, political dynamics, and organizational needs)
- Who could be an immediate interim leader in the event of an incumbent's departure and has he or she been notified?
- Has a key administrator been identified who could manage the transition during the time before replacing the incumbent?
- Has a developmental plan been initiated to help prepare the interim leader for the position?
- Have all potential issues been identified that need to be stabilized during the transition period upon an incumbent's abrupt departure that will ensure operational continuity?

Figure 6.5 outlines the steps for the succession planning process. The first step involves ensuring that a current job description is in place. The job description should be updated to include the organizational role, essential duties and responsibilities, qualifications and requirements, and desired certificates, licenses, or registrations needed for the position. For example, a key position might be the Business Manager of a school district, Principal, Assistant Superintendent for Research and Instructional Development, or Curriculum Specialist.

The second step involves ensuring that the core competencies, which include performance skills, knowledge, and dispositions, have been developed for the key position. Generally these core competencies involve leadership and management skills as well as the actual functional and technical skills needed in the position. For example, core competencies for a position of an Assistant Superintendent for Research and Instructional Development might include technical expertise in understanding research and statistical analysis.

Step three involves working with the school board to ensure that there are agreed-upon expectations for the succession plan. Often a school board may work with an outside consultant to help facilitate the process and provide outside expertise and consultation.

Step four involves identifying and assessing internal and external candidates for the incumbent's position. Promoting internal people may be desired

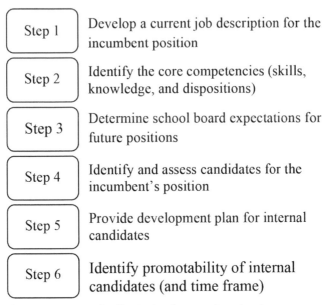

Figure 6.5.   Steps for district-level succession planning process.

to support learning and advancement. However, it may be desirable to bring in fresh people from outside the district. Or, as the saying goes, "a new broom sweeps clean." This will help to ensure a smooth transition in the event of an abrupt departure of an incumbent.

Steps five includes identifying and providing a developmental plan for internal candidates for the position. The capacity for promotion of the candidate, step six, should be determined along with an anticipated time frame from which the candidate could be ready to assume the position.

The core competencies for a position should be identified for a key administrative leadership position. While these core competencies may vary, many of them can be selected from the core competencies presented in earlier chapters. Once the core competencies have been determined, it is then important to identify potential candidates to replace the incumbent and to complete a checklist which can be used. The checklist might also include the following items:

- Promotability—Is the candidate ready to assume the position now or how many years into the future?
- Gap Analysis—The candidate should be evaluated based upon what specific gaps and core competencies are deficient and need to be developed.
- Career Development Plan—Once the gaps have been identified, then specific developmental actions should be completed for the candidate.
- Assigned Mentor—An assigned mentor within the organization should also be responsible for completing the succession planning process and working with the candidates.

The journey in establishing an effective succession plan can be rewarding in many ways. Some examples include promoting collaboration, building honesty and trust, reexamining expectations, assessing performance, brainstorming alternatives for organizational structure, and identifying suitable candidates who can lead the school district in the future. Ultimately, the end result should be a structured and viable succession plan that ensures operational continuity and success.

PROFESSIONAL DEVELOPMENT

One of the most effective strategies in building capacity of the administrative team is through professional development. There are many ways to implement professional development and one viable method, especially for new district team members, is through an effective mentoring program. The superintendent, or senior administrator, can assume the role as the mentor for the new team member. The mentor can also help orientate the new team members to the school district and provide effective coaching.

The selection of dedicated, committed, credible, and experienced school leaders are generally prerequisites for mentors. District mentors should be well trained in how to be an effective coach. Topics might include understanding leadership, instructional improvement, school district operations, budgets and resources, school safety and security, and district policies and procedures. In addition to these professional qualities, an effective mentor needs interpersonal qualities which include being sensitive, a good listener, empathetic, accessible, supportive, honest, and trustworthy.

When working with a new team member a mentor should begin by establishing rapport. He or she should cover the basic job responsibilities, organizational protocol, policies and procedures, budgets, and technology systems. Other items might include dealing with performance issues, handling employee discipline problems, responding to district safety issues, managing resources, and dealing with stakeholder issues.

One of the most important topics to cover with a new team member is time management. The new team member needs to become proficient in multitasking skills. Some of the common time wasters for a new administrator include telephone interruptions, inadequate planning, oversocializing, meetings, procrastinating, dealing with confused responsibilities or expectations, poor communications, and personal disorganization. An effective mentor should coach the new team member on these time wasters and offer strategies for overcoming them.

The mentor should regularly provide casual feedback by asking questions such as "Describe things that are going well for you," "Describe some areas that you would like to improve," "What things can I do as a mentor to better assist you?" The feedback given to new team members by the mentor should be done on a formative versus summative basis. Formative feedback is an ongoing review designed to give informal assessment without the formal supervisory evaluation which becomes part of the new team member's performance record.

For example, if a new team member is experiencing difficulty in handling staff performance and meeting performance expectations, the potential root causes might include: distractions from outside influences, health issues, a poor attitude, need for additional training, or inadequate processes. Besides addressing the issue, the mentor should reinforce the new team member's responsibility for improvement and to provide encouragement for improvement.

Good mentoring may also include asking the new team member for solutions for the performance issue. In this way the person is more likely to accept the solution. It also allows the new team member to take responsibility for his or her own behavior. For example, the new team member may need to include more effective leadership style in leading and managing team performance and accountability.

The mentor and new team member should discuss and agree upon an action plan for resolving any performance issues. There may be some negotiation so they can collaboratively resolve the issue. The new team member might propose a solution that is acceptable to the mentor since he or she will be more apt to accept the solution rather than it being imposed upon him or her.

However, if the new team member's suggestion is unacceptable to the mentor, further discussion may be necessary and ultimately they will need to mutually arrive at an effective action. The mentor should end coaching sessions by thanking the new team member for participating in the sessions and building his or her confidence. Building the confidence of a new team member can have reinforcing consequences.

Other professional development can consist of seminars, cross-training in other departments, and attending conferences. Every employee, regardless if he or she is a new district administrator or staff member, should be involved in professional development. Professional development is an ongoing process and should be mutually designed by district administrators, department chairpersons, and teachers.

Another useful method of building capacity and professional development is through the performance evaluations. The performance evaluation should not be a single-purpose process whereby the supervisor quickly completes a form, holds a brief appraisal session, files the form, and then goes back to business as usual. The superintendent should not consider the performance evaluation as busy work or as a compliance exercise just to satisfy school district or legal requirements.

Performance evaluations can be a mechanism for accomplishing many goals. One reason for the evaluation is to give genuine constructive performance feedback to the team member which can reinforce good performance and identify areas in need of improvement. The review session can also provide an opportunity to motivate employees through intrinsic verbal praise, and a basis for extrinsic rewards such as salary increases and bonuses.

The performance evaluation session can serve to help promote communications, review respective performance, and develop continuous improvement plans for the future. This communication can serve as a basis for further developing people by establishing goals and gaining input that can help the entire organization.

There are many types of performance evaluation systems such as narrative appraisals, formative and summative assessments, 360 rating systems, and goal-based evaluations. Some organizations utilize an open narrative evaluation, especially for high-level administrators and managers. In this system, the subordinate is asked to write a narrative regarding how well he or she performed during the year. This narrative is then used as a basis for the performance review session. This type of system is a more informal approach and promotes communications.

The formative assessment is often used to support the summative evaluation process. During the formative assessment, informal feedback is given to the employee by the supervisor and this information is not used as part of the employee's permanent evaluation record. The whole idea of formative assessment is to give informal feedback without the fear of the information negatively impacting the employee's performance. The summative evaluation is the most popular approach and consists of a combination rating assessment and narrative section on the evaluation form. The evaluation forms can consist of a paper or an electronic copy.

The 360 performance evaluation is a system that uses a multi-rater feedback process to obtain an evaluation on an employee. The feedback is generally provided by multiple supervisors, peers, support staff, community members, and possibly teachers. This system began during the 1950s in the corporate world and gradually gained popularity in school districts. However, the system has been somewhat controversial in that it requires extensive time to collect the feedback and some people feel that the information is not always accurate or used exclusively for developmental purposes.

The 360 feedback may require gaining information from up to four to six people. Each one of these individuals needs to complete an assessment of the employee, which can be time consuming. Sometimes the employee is allowed to choose the raters in addition to the supervisor. There are many decisions to be made in using a 360 approach such as the selection of the type of feedback instrument, number of raters, how the raters are selected, the process to be used, degree of confidentiality, anonymity of the raters, and how to integrate the information into the performance management system.

One advantage of the 360 process is that the employee receives multiple assessments. This may be more valuable than simply obtaining feedback from one supervisor. Also, when feedback is received from multiple stakeholders, a more diverse and comprehensive assessment can be obtained.

BUILDING COLLABORATION

An effective school district leader needs to understand and practice effective leadership and motivation principles and strategies to maximize employee performance. There are many qualities of effective leaders such as technical knowledge and fiscal, interpersonal, training, planning, and coaching skills needed to support the administrative team and achieve the goals of the organization.

Another characteristic of an effective school district leader is that of role modeling. School district leaders often serve as the role model for employees and students and these leaders need to understand and practice good behaviors that support the values of the organization. Good followers often make good leaders. The ability to effectively inspire employees and then to exhibit effective leadership characteristics is critical in modeling these characteristics for employees.

"You can lead a horse to water but you can't make him drink" is a familiar saying that many leaders can relate to. Motivation is a difficult term to define. Essentially it is the willingness of people to partake in an endeavor in order to satisfy their needs. Human beings have an innate desire to satisfy basic physiological and psychological needs.

The ability to influence employees to be motivated to have a desire to achieve a goal should be an objective of educational leaders. While there are many different educational theories regarding motivation, most of them have a common underlying theme regarding the human needs of people. Developing and understanding human needs can be very valuable in motivating employees.

Collaboration and teamwork is a critical synergistic characteristic of most organizations. School district leaders can play an important role in helping an organization create a positive culture of working together to achieve the vision of the school. Therefore, a school district leader's ability to be proactive versus reactive is critical for all administrators. Proactive leadership suggests the leader's ability to anticipate the needs of employees and to take initiative in getting results.

The reactive leader is one who is content with the status quo and does not have the foresight to anticipate employee needs and creates a working environment that is not vibrant and resourceful. A proactive leader is often one who is also service-oriented. This school district leader recognizes his or her role as a leader in providing for the needs of others.

The notion of servant leadership is a moral value that entails a disposition of giving and altruism. The assumption that the leader is serving the needs of others is a key feature of moral and ethical leadership. The concept of moral leadership encourages learning that is based on justice and fairness.

One of the important aspects in managing employees is the school district leader's ability to manage conflict. Leaders often have employees coming into their office with complaints and conflicts with other employees. The leader's ability to effectively manage conflict has a direct relationship with the motivation of employees. There are several sources of conflict in the school district office. Conflict can result from poor communication, roles, territorial issues, goal incongruence, stress, poor procedures and policies, and ineffective leadership.

The perception or actual favoritism given to employees by school district leaders can be a demotivating factor. This perceived or real favoritism is a form of preferential treatment in the eyes of the employee and can lead to disciplinary or performance issues. Administrators often are unaware of the perceived favoritism they may be giving to employees. The perception of favoritism can be as subtle as a mere lack of prolonged eye contact or the inflection of the administrator's voice to certain staff members in a department meeting.

One of the contributors of conflict is that of miscommunication among people. Each interaction with another often involves a negotiating element which leaves room for miscommunication to take place. For example, if a school district leader makes a statement to a teacher and the intention of the message is misunderstood, there may be ill feelings between them. Likewise, miscommunication can take place among administrators.

Some strategies to help school district leaders resolve conflict include: understanding the root cause and context of the conflict, helping people understand that there is more than one viewpoint on a matter, collaborating with the parties by examining areas of agreement and disagreement, and focusing on the conflict issues and avoiding attacking people. The job of the superintendent is one that requires good leadership and collaboration (Tomal & Schilling, 2013).

SUMMARY

Strategic planning and succession planning are key responsibilities of a superintendent in maintaining and building capacity of the organization. The professional development and evaluation of team members is one that requires a systematic and comprehensive knowledge in all aspects of district leadership. The proper mentoring and professional development of team members can help improve student achievement and contribute to high morale in the organization. Moreover, incorporating an effective performance evaluation system can help ensure that team members perform to the standards required by the organization and allow the school district to be legally compliant.

Building collaboration and teamwork are critical for an effective district-level leadership team. Employing effective leadership and motivation strategies can help to achieve successful teamwork. Moreover, developing a collaborative approach with involvement by all stakeholders can help to ensure agreement and success in building capacity and motivation and morale of all district members.

CASE STUDY

You have been recently hired as the school district superintendent for Johnson School District 203 in northwestern United States. The school has approximately 2,000 students and a teaching faculty which is fairly diverse in age, race, and gender. The academic performance of the students is average as compared to other school districts in the state. The school district does not have a current strategic plan.

As a new superintendent:

1. Outline how you would go about developing a strategic plan for the district.
2. Describe what might be four to six major goals (themes or areas) that you might consider.
3. How would you go about ensuring that everyone has involvement or an understanding of the strategic plan?
4. Outline a plan to ensure effective follow-up and evaluation of the strategic plan.

EXERCISES AND DISCUSSION QUESTIONS

1. Outline an effective succession planning program for a school district including who should be involved in this process.
2. Describe an effective mentoring program at the school district level and how you might implement this program.
3. Describe how you would ensure a viable accountability program for the performance of your school district team.

REFERENCES

Cal State LA's Strategic Plan. (2016). 2016 strategic planning process. Cal State LA. Retrieved from http://www.calstatela.edu/strategicplan/2016-strategic-planning-process.

Connerly, B. (March 24, 2014). The death of strategic planning: Why? *Forbes*. Retrieved from http://www.forbes.com/sites/billconerly/2014/03/24/the-death-of-strategic-planning-why/#35195bdb2f7c.

Larcker, D., & Saslow, S. (2014). *The 2014 report on senior executive succession planning and talent development.* Rock Center for Corporate Governance. Stanford Graduate School of Business. Stanford, CA.

Tomal, D., & Schilling, C. (2013). *Managing human resources and collective bargaining.* Lanham, MD: Rowman & Littlefield.

Chapter Seven

Dollars and Sense

The Superintendent as Steward

OBJECTIVES

At the conclusion of this chapter you will be able to:

1. Understand the concept of stewardship as it relates to the superintendent's role in school districts (ELCC 1; PSEL 1).
2. Understand the variables involved in making financial decisions to improve student outcomes (ELCC 1, 2, 3; PSEL 1, 9, 10).
3. Recognize the attributes of a well-managed organization with respect to financial decision-making (ELCC 3; PSEL 1, 9).
4. Understand the concepts of fiscal integrity and accountability (ELCC 1, 3; PSEL 1, 9).
5. Articulate how effectiveness and efficiency should be used to allocate funds in a school district (ELCC 1, 2, 3; PSEL 1, 9).

WHAT IS BEING A STEWARD?

A wise school board president once remarked "money is never a satisfier, it is only a dissatisfier." Unfortunately, there is more truth to this statement than fiction. Wealthy districts work to protect what they have and poor districts work to acquire more. While research is mixed on how much money makes a difference, a superintendent has to be realistic. A superintendent has to work with what is available but advocate for what is needed.

The traditional definition of fiscal stewardship in public schools is the duty to spend taxpayer money wisely. Many, however, would argue that that definition

111

of stewardship no longer adequately addresses what is expected today. Today's definition would include the duty to ensure the:

1. fiscal integrity of the school district,
2. efficient and effective use of resources, and
3. attainment of student outcomes through sound financial decision-making.

Superintendents also have to ensure that they are maintaining fiscal integrity, addressing student outcomes, and effectively using resources. The concept of fiscal integrity has been around a long time. Traditionally, it has referred to an obligation to ensure that funds are used wisely and legally. Associating student outcomes and resource allocation is a relatively new concept. The issue has come to the forefront, as more and more districts must assess the impact and the effectiveness of resources. What further complicates the idea of stewardship in schools is the diversity of their major stakeholders. Those groups include students, taxpayers, and staff. Figure 7.1 shows the relationship of fiscal integrity, efficiency and effectiveness, and student outcomes.

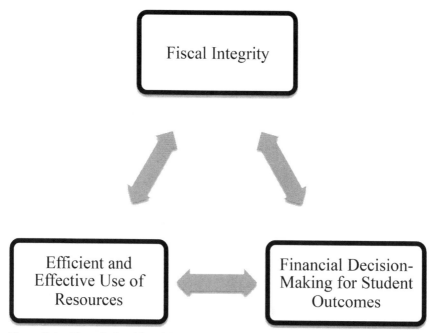

Figure 7.1.   The relationship of fiscal integrity, student outcomes, and efficiency and effectiveness.

Superintendents must balance the needs of each major stakeholder group. Focusing on taxpayers, for example, may result in low staff salaries, a lack of technology, or an absence of funding for improving instruction and student outcomes. On the other hand, focusing on items of importance to staff such as low class size and high salaries may result in fiscal commitments that are unsustainable. Focusing strictly on students is also not without its issues. Doing so may result in a curriculum and activities that are unsustainable and expensive. The challenge is to find that delicate balance where the needs of all stakeholders are being met.

FISCAL INTEGRITY

Every state has "rules of the road" for the fiscal operations of school districts. It is incumbent on superintendents to become familiar with the legal requirements for procuring and managing resources for their school districts. Depending on the size of the district, superintendents may also be responsible for overseeing the day-to-day functions of the business office. Every superintendent has a fiduciary responsibility to safeguard the resources of the district. It does not matter whether those resources are in the form of taxpayer dollars, money raised by students, payments collected from parents, or assets such as facilities.

As CEOs, superintendents cannot spend all their time overseeing the business functions of a school district. To provide proper oversight, they must educate themselves as to the measures necessary to minimize the misappropriate use of funds or assets of the district. Superintendents should realize that good fiscal oversight does not prevent irregularities but it does greatly diminish their chances of occurring. Following is a brief discussion of some of the steps a superintendent can take to safeguard the funds and assets of a district:

Stay Engaged. Simply, do not turn over the fiscal operations of the district to someone else and walk away. Chief executive officers (CEOs) at any level need to maintain a keen interest in fiscal operations, including asking critical questions about the financial reports including budgets, periodic financial statements, and audited financial statements.

Employ Qualified Staff. If the district can afford a full- or part-time school business official, then one should be employed. Most states do not have certification requirements or educational programs for school business officials. However, there are state associations for school business officials which are a good source when looking for a qualified school business manager or even for obtaining training.

Sometimes, the most difficult decision is deciding whom to hire. Districts employ a wide range of individuals in the chief school business role. The evolution of the position requires both technical expertise and a collaborative personality to work with both administrators and teachers. Candidates with business and education backgrounds can fill the role. Either will work with the right disposition and skill set.

Segregate Duties. Fraud occurs more often in districts that either can't or don't segregate duties. For example, one employee should not issue purchase orders, approve invoices, and write the checks. Likewise, whoever pays teachers should not have access to their contracts. In larger districts this isn't usually an issue.

In smaller ones, segregation of duties may not be able to be achieved to the extent possible in large districts. Using the first example, in small districts, the first person may issue the purchase order, a second individual approves the invoice, and the first person writes the check. Although not ideal, the duties have now been split between two staff members and therefore fraud would be more difficult because it would require the collusion of two people.

Establish Internal Controls. Establishing procedures that safeguard funds and assets is critical to good fiscal management. This would include the segregation of duties mentioned above as well as the review, authorization, and reconciliation of transactions. Internal controls can be either preventative or investigative. Preventive controls would include the differentiation of duties, clear policies and procedures, reconciling records, reviewing purchase orders, and management review.

Investigative controls would include those things that tend to minimize risk such as exception reports, inventories of assets, or reconciling the general ledger to bank statements. A number of states have internal control manuals for school districts that superintendents can utilize. Auditors are another source of assistance in determining the appropriateness of the internal controls a district is using.

Financial Reporting. Financial reports and source documents provide assurances that transactions are appropriately documented, accurately reflected in the general ledger, and compliant with laws, regulations, and other requirements. Superintendents should require regular, timely, and complete financial reports from internal finance staff or contract staff and expect the board to hold staff accountable for meeting the standards of timely reporting (for example, providing financial statements no later than three weeks after the close of the prior accounting period).

Risk Management. Risk management can take many forms. Basically, there are three approaches to managing risk: insure it, avoid it, or transfer it. Most school districts insure risk by purchasing insurance directly from a provider or through participating in an insurance pool. Districts can avoid risk by simply not allowing the activities with additional risk such as ski trips or trampolines.

Having the school district being named as an additional insured on contracts is the most common form of transferring risk. These might include food service, transportation, construction, or other vendor contracts. Surety and performance bonds should be used when legally required or where there are significant contract obligations. Last but not least, districts should require an analytics and prevention component to all insurance contracts. The analytics identifies areas of concern and the prevention component mitigates losses.

Facilities Management. Facilities are often "the elephant in the room." Many districts struggle to keep their facilities up to date. During times of limited resources, facilities projects are often the first to be cut in favor of staff obligations and maintaining instructional programs. Most states have health and life safety standards for educational facilities. There is no substitute for a good facilities team. That team would include district management, an architect, and possibly other professionals such as a demographer. The key to maintaining facilities is to have a plan.

A facilities plan should focus on short- and long-term needs. A typical plan would show needs for each of the next five years and then a total for the following five years. It would be evaluated and updated annually. Failure to maintain facilities puts districts at financial risk. If every dollar is obligated for instructional programs and services, the only source of revenue to address a significant facilities need is to repurpose operating dollars.

EFFICIENT AND EFFECTIVE USE OF RESOURCES

The public should never have to pay for inefficiency. To figure out what schools need to spend, they first need to determine what students should be expected to know. Generally, the rule of thumb is that change is more effective at the school level but costlier since it is customized to each building's needs and culture. Effectiveness is making sure resources produce the results (outcomes) desired. Efficiency is making sure the minimum resources are spent to be effective. The terms are not mutually exclusive. In a school, this is tying resources to student performance. Figure 7.2 illustrates the linkage between efficiency and effectiveness.

For most school districts, financial resources are limited. For this reason, efficiency is not about creating new programs, strategies, and organizations that require more financial resources but creating those opportunities through the repurposing of current resources. It becomes essential that the school

Figure 7.2. The linkage between efficiency and effectiveness with regard to cost and achievement.

community have good data from which to evaluate each component of its organization from the classroom to the district office. There is no recent change in education more impactful on school finance than the emerging focus on analytics to evaluate student outcomes.

As CEOs, superintendents are constantly challenged to meet the academic and socializing needs for the students they serve. Whereas private businesses seek to minimize overhead and increase profits, public schools tend to maximize the utilization of budgets in support of increasing achievement. In economically challenged times, businesses reduce expenses and increase efficiency to stay in business and attempt to stay profitable. For businesses, productivity is the key.

School districts are not used to thinking in terms of productivity. Schools tend to think of efficiency as simply making "cuts" to balance their budget.

However, making certain "cuts" can be counterproductive. Basically, there are only three methods of balancing a school budget: cut spending; increase revenues, or a combination of both (Wong & Casing, 2010).

Core and Non-Core Functions

Operations of a school can be divided into two categories: core and non-core functions. Core functions relate to teaching and learning while non-core functions relate to support services such as transportation, food service, custodial/maintenance, security, etc. The goal for any district should be to deliver non-core functions as effectively and efficiently as possible in order to allocate as many resources as possible to core functions. Some districts do this through using their own staff—others through outsourcing. In either case, the administrative role is the same. This is important since the biggest mistake most districts make when they outsource is not retaining some type of administrative oversight.

The fact is that most start-up businesses fail. Consequently, it is important to evaluate the use of resources with respect to implementing change in a classroom, department, school, district, or, for that matter, any educational environment. Change should always be viewed as a pilot. Some changes fail while others do not.

How is the success of a change evaluated? The first step is to start with the definition of excellence. The definition may include tangible or intangible benchmarks. It may be a change in test scores or behavior. As simple as it may sound, increasing the attendance at school may be indicative of success. A student's willingness to attend school may be reflective of a change in school culture that values every child. Likewise, growth in academic achievement may be seen as success.

The key to both these examples is the magnitude of the change (effectiveness) and the resource commitment (efficiency) to effect the change. Textbox 7.1 is an illustration of a form for evaluating new staff proposals. Note that the left side of the illustration basically describes the proposal resource requirements while the right side identifies the estimated costs.

With this background, what factors need to be reviewed to conclude whether or not a change was effective and efficient? How is it that efficiency is not always achieved on the first attempt at change factored into the equation? A large initial investment, either in terms of financial resources or personnel time, may be required to implement the change. Over time, fewer resources may be needed. Likewise, as staff becomes familiar and comfortable with the change, its effectiveness may improve. For these reasons, it is not only important to set a definition of excellence but also to estimate how long it will take to achieve.

Textbox 7.1. Illustration of a Form for Evaluating New Staff Proposals					
Proposal Name	Reading Improvement Grades 1–3				
Number of Students Impacted: 130			Is this a Pilot Study: Y/N N		
Resource Requirements:	Salaries	Benefits	Supplies	Equipment	TOTAL
Staffing	45,000	4,000			49,000
Professional Development	7,500	750			8,250
New Textbooks			11,000		11,000
Tablet Computers				10,000	10,000
TOTAL (in dollars)	52,500	4,750	11,000	10,000	78,250
Estimated Cost per Student	$602 per student				
Are any of resources required being repurposed from other proposals?	Tablets from science				
Evaluation Methodology	Growth in reading over next school year				
Definition of success (growth, score, % attaining competency, etc.)	5% improvement in students meeting state standards				

Evaluating any change is always difficult. The first step in the process is to review the data. Data may be standardized test scores, interviews, behavioral assessments, surveys, or other appropriate instruments. Was the definition of excellence achieved? Was it completed within the time frame anticipated? Were there any unintended consequences? Many times making one change may have unforeseen impacts—good or bad. A change in a professional development strategy to increase math comprehension may also lead to higher levels of parental satisfaction with the school. On the other hand, attempts to implement a new tardy policy may result in more absences if the consequence of multiple instances of tardiness is perceived by students to be more onerous than just missing a class.

Unintended consequences need to be evaluated to make sure any negative effects do not outweigh any positive effects of the change. An assessment of the resources used needs to be completed. Were the resources required within the acceptable parameters projected by the school or organization? Was the change efficient? Do the data show that a more efficient strategy may be available? During the process did the school discover any alternatives that should be explored? Last, but not least, is the change sustainable? Unless a change is designed to address a specific short-term goal, are there enough resources to sustain the change over time?

One of the mistakes districts make when implementing new programs is not considering the value proposition of the change. This is especially true when it comes to resources. Without adequate resources, change becomes a burden instead of an opportunity. In order to evaluate a change from both an efficiency and effectiveness perspective, districts would be well served to view it from a value proposition model.

In most organizations a pilot study is simply a test with a pass/fail grade. In a value proposition model there is no grade—it is a learning model based on continuous improvement and evaluation (see figure 7.3). The key to the value

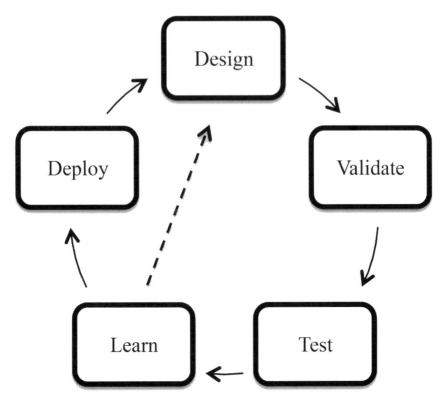

Figure 7.3.   Steps in the value proposition model.

proposition model is what happens at the end of the normal cycle. It does not stop. It is continuous. It starts with a design or plan. After design there is validation. Validation involves confirming the design through research. Next is testing—a small pilot.

Upon completion of the small pilot the "What has been learned?" question is asked. If value has been realized (i.e., success, effectiveness, and efficiency), deployment can take place. If the pilot was unsuccessful, then the deployment phase should be skipped. Staff has two options based on what has been learned: 1) either terminate the initiative, or 2) continue the initiative but put it back through the entire cycle. This step can be repeated as many times as necessary to ensure the initiative is successful. If deployment does occur, the cycle continues. In other words, the cycle keeps repeating itself. This ensures that every initiative will be continuously evaluated, redesigned, validated, and tested.

In order for school districts to be successful and efficient in how they distribute resources, they need to understand they will be unsuccessful. Staff may follow all the steps, implement the process, and still find that the initiative is just not effective. From a leadership perspective, superintendents have to create a culture where failure is acceptable as long as it leads to success. This will encourage teacher-driven initiatives and entrepreneurship—both of which are important to school improvement (Schilling, 2006).

FINANCIAL DECISION-MAKING
FOR STUDENT OUTCOMES

Intuitively, educators would all like to think that the more resources a district receives, the higher its students will perform. Unfortunately, a review of literature on the link between resources and student performance still generates more questions than answers. Even so, it is apparent that the future is clearly focused on student outcomes. This will inevitably lead to greater discussion on the alignment of financial resources with student outcomes. This will encourage further research on the most productive and efficient ways to use resources for enhancing student performance. It will be crucial that superintendents understand these relationships.

In order to increase student performance, outcomes and resources have to be aligned. One of the key ingredients in any model for improving student performance and outcomes is having adequate resources. That means that resources need to be:

- targeted based on research and best practices,
- allocated based on professional control and input, and
- evaluated based on their effectiveness on student outcomes.

Simply put "How should resources be spent based on research and practice, cost effectiveness, and their impact on the outcomes for all students?"

Adams and Evans (2008) suggest that there are some inherent problems with the current way that finance systems target and link resources. They looked at five different attributes of financing systems: the resource target, the linkage between resources and educational programs, the resource management process, accountability, and the link between resources and student outcomes. They observed that in conventional finance systems resources are directed toward district goals. Furthermore, they concluded that in conventional finance systems there is no link between resources and education programs; spending is governed by categories; accountability is a matter of compliance; and the link between resources and outcomes is missing.

Aligning Fiscal Resources

There are several steps a superintendent can take to ensure that resources are aligned to educational programs and student outcomes. The first step is to ensure the district has a solid budget policy. The budget is, by definition, the blueprint for how a district is going to allocate its resources. It should address the budget process, priorities, and reserve goals. The policy should be clear as to the priorities of the district (see textbox 7.2). If fiscal challenges

---

Textbox 7.2. Sample Budget Policy Priorities

The superintendent or his designee shall utilize the following guidelines in developing the budget unless otherwise modified by the board of education:

1. The budget shall first provide for staff and operating expenses to meet projected changes in student enrollment and mandated programs.
2. The budget shall reflect the board of education's desire to maintain the overall tax rate of the district when possible.
3. The budget shall reflect the board of education's desire to not increase the overall indebtedness of the district.
4. The budget shall reflect the board of education's desire to maintain safe and operationally sound facilities.
5. The budget shall anticipate compliance with all applicable governmental and legal obligations of the district.
6. The budget shall include a reasonable contingency for variable and unanticipated costs.
7. The administrative team shall, in connection with the preliminary budget, identify potential efficiencies from interbuilding, interdepartmental, and district-wide coordination or from building or district program or other organizational restructuring initiatives.

occur, it is much easier to address them if the district has already established its priorities.

An astute superintendent will ensure that the planning cycles for finance, instruction, facilities, etc. run parallel to each other so that needs can be strategically prioritized. That also means identifying the strategies available for achieving those outcomes. Outcomes include not only those related to the academic performance of students but the fiscal health of the organization and maintenance of a safe and secure learning environment. Following are some suggested steps in this process (Schilling, 2010):

- Establish broad goals
- Establish financial parameters
- Confirm educational needs
- Confirm facilities needs
- Develop approaches and strategies
- Make choices

Establish Broad Goals. The goal of every superintendent should be to provide student equity over time and have a means of measuring it. Establishing broad goals that promote sustainability and scalable success in student performance over time is crucial to allocating resources. The natural inclination for most school districts is to address the most immediate needs of the organization. This, of course, ignores planning for long-term success.

Financially, this may be as simple as ensuring that expenditures for instruction are adjusted annually based on enrollment and the cost of living. Academically, it may mean developing criteria to ensure that test scores and student outcomes are met over time. This is especially important when addressing the needs of students from low-income families, English learners, and students with disabilities, to shield them from the impact of budget reductions. The key to establishing broad goals is the involvement of all stakeholders in the process. Collaborative and meaningful engagement of all stakeholders is important in ensuring the successful implementation of goals.

Establish Financial Parameters. Each school and school district needs to establish its own financial parameters. Financial parameters provide a basis for how funds are to be distributed as well as benchmarks for the fiscal well-being of the district. How a budget is developed and who is responsible for deciding how resources are allocated is an important decision. No matter how much the board, superintendent, and other central office administrators are involved, the ultimate decision is made at the school building level. School personnel know where resources are needed and are responsible for achieving the goals of the school. A significant portion of the resource allocation authority should reside with the principal and his/her staff.

Data-driven resource models are just as important at the school and school district level as they are at the state level. Ensuring intradistrict equity and adequacy for students and schools creates a level playing field. Simply dispersing funds based on the number of students in each school does not serve the best interests of anyone. The method of dispersing funds should depend on the make-up of the student body and the challenges instructing them pose. This would include language barriers and socioeconomic class.

Confirm Educational Needs. Confirming educational needs is important in that it forces an organization to reevaluate programs in light of student outcomes. School districts tend to maintain programs already in existence and have difficulty eliminating those that no longer are effective. Demographics change as well as best practices and student needs. Confirming educational needs is like getting an annual physical. It is a preventative, proactive measure. The result of such a process is that resources can be repurposed to promote student outcomes and other district goals.

An organization's current educational needs can be determined through a number of approaches. Among these are reviewing data which shed light on which practices, programs, processes, and policies have been effective in producing measurable improvements in student outcomes. Simply put, invest in what works. This is especially important in times of limited educational resources. Shifting resources from less effective to more effective programs and strategies will most likely result in the least amount of harm to students.

Confirm Facility Needs. Facilities are an integral part of the operation of a school or school district. Other than instructional and support services, maintaining facilities can be a significant cost to school districts. In times of financial restraint and challenges, schools often settle for just "doing the minimum." Unfortunately, that can have devastating consequences for a school district in the long-term. Not fixing a water leak now for $35,000 may result in a $500,000 mold problem in a year or two.

Another consideration in any renovation of school facilities is what changes can be incorporated to save energy costs. Not all savings are equal. The key indicator of whether or not to include these is the "payback period." The payback period refers to the length of time that the cost of the energy savings improvement takes to pay for itself. For example, a project with a cost of $200,000 with an annual savings of $20,000 would take ten years to pay for itself.

Develop Approaches and Strategies. Education Resource Strategies, Inc. has developed five strategies to assist low-performing schools in improving their chances for success (Baroody, 2011). Those strategies are:

1. Understand what each school needs.
2. Quantify what each school gets and how it is used.
3. Invest in the most important changes first.
4. Customize the strategy to the school.
5. Change the district, not just the school.

Although these strategies were developed for low-performing schools they have applicability for all schools. All schools are different. Distributing resources based on a custom solution for each school has merit. Most states require school not district improvement plans. Later in this chapter other strategies and models will also be explored.

Making Choices. If there is one thing that school districts sometimes struggle with, it's making difficult choices. Who wants to pick increased class size over band or vice versa? The key is to trust the existing process and the research that has been done. Often there is research which supports multiple positions. Two more students per class in a large district might result in a dozen more teachers that could be utilized for coaching and mentoring, a new technology, or an updated science curriculum.

Allocating and Managing Resources

In a time of limited resources, site-based, school-based, or student-centric budgeting models have gained popularity. Most of these resource allocation models presume, in some part, that the most efficient use of resources results when building-level staff are empowered to prioritize and allocate how resources are spent. The key to any of these models is ensuring that everyone in the chain of command believes in the process. The impact is lost if any administrative level fails to collaborate with their stakeholders: teachers and department chairs, department chairs and principals, and the superintendent with principals.

Superintendents are constantly challenged to lead staff in meeting the desired academic and socializing outcomes for the students they serve. How do superintendents ensure that resources are allocated appropriately to obtain those goals? According to Daggett (2009), school districts need to focus "resources and accountability around specific tools, strategies, professional development, procedures, and policies that can be documented to improve student performance." He goes on to state that this is a subtle change that shifts the focus from inputs (programs) to outputs (student performance).

Incorporating resource allocation strategies is crucial to help staff improve their chances for success. It's not about the math or reading program. It's about a student's performance in reading or math. Change is more likely to occur in budgeting systems where schools have control over human as well as financial resources and have the authority to make decisions about how those resources will be allocated. In other words, a sense of ownership and leadership is important throughout the organization to ensure resources are targeted to be the most impactful.

There are two types of change for which resources need to be allocated and managed. The first is a pedagogical change, such as would be typical in a routine curriculum review. The second is a structural change, such as changing class size standards. Pedagogical change requires transition as well as implementation and evaluation resources for the proposed change. Transitional resources are one-time costs associated with planning and preparing for the change. Implementation resources are those costs associated with executing the change and include capital outlay, instructional materials, professional development, and technology. Evaluation resources include the cost of technology and personnel to administer online tests, proctors, assessments, consultants, and other specialized services.

Public school districts have experimented with various forms of budget organization to manage resources. Line item and function/object budgeting are basic to almost all systems. What varies from district to district and school to school is the methodology used to distribute resources through the budgeting and financial planning process (Cooper & Nisonoff, 2002). William Hartman, author of *School District Budgeting* (1999), defines education budgeting as a "working tool" for the successful operation of states and local school districts, and as a "significant opportunity to plan the mission, improve their operations, and achieve their education objectives." As such, the budgeting process provides districts the opportunity to "make better financial and program decisions, improve operations, and enhance relations with citizens and other stakeholders" (National Advisory Council on State and Local Budgeting, 1995, p. 2).

Many superintendents are well-versed in instructional methodology and organizational theory. However, it is often a constant struggle to effectively manage the budget and finances of the school (Cooper, 2011). To some, budgeting may seem too complicated. For others it may be a lack of education or simply a lack of time. A budget is a means of communicating to the public, parents, and staff the values of a district.

The purpose of prioritizing the budgeting process is to bring spending into alignment with policy priorities. It also eliminates repetition of services, establishes economies of scale, and creates parameters for downsizing. The point of allocating and budgeting resources is not to change for the sake of change. The goal of allocating and budgeting resources should be to assist staff in implementing what the stakeholders in a district expect of their schools.

Regardless of what form of budgeting a school system uses, superintendents must insist that resources be allocated based on research, results, or legal compliance. In other words, it must be based on some type of evidence. Getting all stakeholders together to determine the distribution of funds within a department, school, or district requires not only a significant time commitment, but also knowledge of how resources impact student outcomes.

The student-centric budgeting (SCB) model is an approach to educational resource allocation and budgeting that is based on identifying student needs and aligning resources to give schools the tools they need to be successful (Schilling, 2013). This approach is extremely suited to teacher-led change and distributed leadership.

The central theme of this model is that teacher quality is the single most important ingredient in improving student achievement. Having staff that understand student needs and the centric model includes the following strategies:

- Understand what students need to achieve (data).
- Find research-supported approaches to meeting student needs (interventions).
- Quantifying what teachers need to meet student needs (resources).
- Investing in strategies that return the greatest gains in student performance (efficiency).
- Customizing instructional strategies to each teacher (instruction).
- Evaluating the success of the strategies (outcomes).

SCB can have other benefits besides resource allocation and management. It can be used as an accountability process as well as a basis for encouraging grass roots innovation and entrepreneurship in schools.

Understanding what students need to achieve (data) involves mining the data, analyzing them, and establishing action plans. The data needed will depend on the type of change desired: pedagogical or structural. Pedagogical change will most likely require standardized testing data. Structural change, such as adding staff, will most likely need to include other leadership.

Finding research-supported approaches to meeting student needs (interventions) must be based on an understanding of what students need to achieve (data). Interventions should be viewed from many possible perspectives. Interventions can be anything, from a simple change in a textbook to pulling students out of the classroom for additional help. They may be either pedagogical or structural in nature. In either case, interventions require change from the status quo.

Quantifying what teachers need to meet student needs (resources) involves establishing what resources are needed for teachers to be successful. Superintendents need to think in terms of targeting resources to schools as opposed to system-wide programs. Teachers are resource managers at the most basic level. If a teacher finds that students are failing to learn with one text, then they need to have the resources to provide a different book. Determining what teachers need requires that districts be able to distinguish between individual and group needs. In either case, the key is to match resources with needs. This requires the cooperation of all teachers. This is about allowing those closest to the instructional process to set priorities and allocate funds.

Investing in strategies that return the greatest gains in student performance (efficiency) seems simple but it is actually hard to do. This step requires assessment and research. For example, let's assume that a superintendent has the following choice: they can implement a one-on-one technology strategy across the curriculum or add one additional teacher facilitator to each grade level. Which strategy is more effective? Which will generate the greatest gains in student achievement? How do superintendents arrive at the best decision?

Customizing instructional strategies to each teacher (instruction) is critical for them to be successful. Districts do this through the process of coaching and mentoring staff and providing them with the appropriate resources. Just as no two students learn in the same way, neither do teachers teach the same way.

Evaluating the success of the strategies (outcomes) involves collecting data and comparing the actual results against what was expected. Strategies that are unsuccessful or marginally unsuccessful should be reviewed to see if they are worth continuing. Furthermore, consideration should be given as to how efficient a particular strategy was versus the incremental results obtained. It is important to look at each step in the process. A breakdown in one step can lead to failures in others. Textbox 7.3 indicates the roles superintendents have for each step in the student-centric model.

The challenges of any allocation model are: 1) including all groups—from special education through gifted including English learners (EL), 2) providing some discretionary money for every school, and 3) addressing students

---

Textbox 7.3.   The Role Superintendents Have in the Student-Centric Budgeting Model

Works with staff to understand what students need to achieve desired outcomes.

Insists on research-based approaches to meet student outcomes.

Encourages grass roots innovation and entrepreneurship.

Insists that transition, implementation, and evaluative resources are identified for new initiatives.

Insists on efficiency—target strategies that produce the greatest gains.

Ensures that strategies are customized based on school and teacher needs.

Evaluates outcomes as a learning strategy for continous improvement.

---

with multiple challenges such as EL, low-income, or at-risk. No matter what, the result will probably be a reduction in resources for that middle student.

Obviously, the real questions here are: 1) from a staff perspective do they believe they can make better decisions than the district office about how funds are targeted, and 2) where do parents put their trust—is it in the district office or the school? The truth is probably somewhere in-between. Schools need discretion but they also need to be accountable.

As a superintendent, the budget should be a reflection of the academic priorities, goals, and objectives for students. Academic initiatives like the Common Core will have an effect on how many school districts allocate funds. Putting in place systems that measure the effectiveness and efficiency of resources in increasing student performance is crucial to the success of the Common Core.

SUMMARY

The role of the school superintendent has evolved significantly over the last century. One of the emerging roles for the school superintendent is stewardship. Stewardship in the twenty-first century is multifaceted. It includes safeguarding funds, efficiency, and effectiveness. In today's economy, superintendents must find ways to repurpose funds from non-core functions to core functions.

Safeguarding resources can be accomplished through a number of strategies. They include active engagement, financial reporting, and employing qualified personnel and establishing good internal controls. Proactive financial oversight will greatly reduce the probability of fraud or the misuse of district funds.

Linking financial decisions to student outcomes accomplishes two important things. First, it ensures there is alignment between how funds are spent and student outcomes. Second, it puts student outcomes at the center of resource allocation decisions. There are a variety of approaches to aligning and allocating resources. The student-centric budgeting model emphasizes a custom approach, which centers on the teacher and school as resource managers.

The public expects efficient and effective schools. With the rise in analytics data available to taxpayers, parents, and staff, superintendents are under the microscope not only for student but also for fiscal performance. Most districts do not have unlimited resources which means that efficiency is important in that it allows for the repurposing of funds from non-core to core functions like teaching and learning.

CASE STUDY

After several attempts, Kim finally gets her chance to be a superintendent of a small elementary school district with about 1,000 students. The district is composed of two K–8 buildings with about 75 staff members. Because of its size, the district does not have a business manager. One of Kim's first tasks is to finish the budget for the district and submit it to the State Board of Education. After she enters everything a "red flag" pops up and says, "deficit reduction plan required."

Since Kim is new she calls a consultant who was recommended to her. Much to her surprise he says the district is going broke. The $6 million in reserves the district had several years ago are now down to $3 million and the district is deficit spending at the rate of $1.2 million per year on an $11 million budget. The district will be out of money in three years at that rate. The consultant goes on to say, the district must submit a deficit reduction plan that shows how it will balance its budget in three years—that is, eliminate the $1.2 million in deficit spending.

Can Kim do this by herself or does she need help? How does Kim communicate the news to the various stakeholders? How does Kim go about addressing the need for either more revenue or substantial reductions? Who should Kim involve—in and outside the district—to help her formulate a game plan?

EXERCISES AND DISCUSSION QUESTIONS

1. You are a new superintendent in a small elementary district. Your only staff is a secretary and payroll/bookkeeper. Describe your strategy for safeguarding the funds of the district. What will be your first steps? What

challenges or obstacles do you anticipate and do you have a strategy for overcoming them?

2. In a recent election, three of the board members ran on a fiscal account-ability platform. All three believe there is no relationship between what the district spends and what students achieve. Consequently, they want to trim the budget and "give taxpayers a break." How do you convince the board members the district needs the funds it receives and is spending them wisely? Describe your strategy for establishing and cultivating a positive relationship with the three new members.

3. The board of education has asked you to propose procedures for new programs to present to them for approval. They want a complete process—from the time a new program is considered until it is tentatively approved for a pilot student until it receives final board approval for deployment. What process will you utilize? What will be your key decision points in the process? Who will be involved in deciding which new programs will be presented for board approval? How will you communicate the key features of your plan to the staff?

4. You are a newly appointed superintendent promoted to the position after five years in the district as principal. As soon as the first budget cycle starts, the board indicates it wants to be more involved in deciding how resources are allocated to the school buildings. After some discussion, they ask you for advice as to how they can be more involved. What advice would you give the board? What is the proper role of a board in the budget allocation process?

5. After becoming the superintendent of a large elementary district, the union president approaches you regarding the district's fiscal operations. She indicates that although the district has had a pretty good record of adequately allocating resources to each building, the teachers have had little say in how the funds are spent. She indicates the principals in the district have always controlled the "purse strings" with little input from the staff. Furthermore, she indicates that this will be a major negotiating issue the next time the two sides are at the table if something doesn't happen. How would you go about changing the culture at the school sites? More specifically, how would you go about changing the resource management habits of the principals?

REFERENCES

Adams, J. E., & Evans, D. J. (2008). *Funding student learning: How to align educa-tion resources with student learning goals.* National Working Group on Funding Student Learning. Seattle: University of Washington, Center on Reinventing Public Education.

Baroody, K. (2011, February 4). Turning around the nation's lowest performing schools: Five steps districts can take to improve their chances of success. *Center for American Progress*. Retrieved from http://www.americanprogress.org/issues/2011/02/five_steps.html.

Cooper, B., & Nisonoff, P. (2002). Public school budgeting, accounting, and auditing. *Encyclopedia of Education*. The Gale Group. Retrieved from http://www.encyclopedia.com/education/encyclopedias-almanacs-transcripts-maps/public-school-budgeting-accounting-and-auditing.

Cooper, K. (2011). Budgeting based on results. *Education Digest 76*(9): 4–8.

Daggett, W. (2009, April). Effectiveness and efficiency framework: A guide to focusing on student performance. International Center for Leadership in Education. Retrieved from http://www.leadered.com/pdf/effectiveness_efficiency_framework_2014.pdf.

Hartman, W. (1999). *School district budgeting.* Reston, VA: Association of School Business Officials International.

National Advisory Council on State and Local Budgeting (NACSLB). (1995). *A framework for improved state and local budgeting and recommended budgeting practices.* Chicago: Government Finance Officers Association.

National Education Association. (1987). *Understanding state school finance formulas.* National Education Association. West Haven, CT: NEA Professional Library.

Schilling, C. (2006, November). Entrepreneurship in education. Paper presented at the Jamaican Association of School Bursars Annual Meeting, Jamaica.

———. (2010, March). Funding our vision: A five-year plan to provide excellence and opportunity for all. Presentation to West Northfield School District 31, Northbrook, IL.

———. (2013). The school business manager as a change agent. Presentation to the Association of School Business Officials International, Boston.

Wong, O. K., & Casing, D. M. (2010). *Equalize student achievement: Prioritizing money and power.* Lanham, MD: Rowman & Littlefield Education.

Chapter Eight

Seeing the Forest for the Trees

Benchmarking District Performance

OBJECTIVES

At the conclusion of this chapter you will be able to:

1. Understand the importance of gauging district performance (ELCC 1, 3; PSEL 1, 4, 6, 7, 9).
2. Recognize and utilize indicators to assess district performance (ELCC 1, 3; PSEL 1, 4, 6, 7, 9).
3. Identify what performance and operational audits are and how they can be used to effectively manage and improve performance (ELCC 1; PSEL 4, 9, 10).
4. Understand the importance and role of analytics (ELCC 1, 3, 4; PSEL 4, 9, 10).
5. Effectively utilize performance indicators, performance and operational audits, and analytics to implement change (ELCC 1, 3, 6; PSEL 1, 9).

GAUGING DISTRICT PERFORMANCE

The job of a superintendent can be daunting. It is the combination of a football quarterback and center positions rolled into one. The quarterback has to see the whole field while the center has to make the right calls to protect key players. Superintendents have both of these responsibilities—to implement the vision and to make the right management calls.

The classroom and school are important intervention points for improving student achievement. In fact, most states require school improvement plans in one form or another. But what critical factors distinguish successful school

133

districts from those that are less successful? What is the role of superintendent in promoting district improvement and success? Most importantly, how do stakeholders gauge the performance of school districts? Since the superintendent is the leader of the school district, the success of the district and superintendent almost always go hand-in-hand. So what strategies are there for the superintendent to gauge how the district is doing?

There are a number of approaches that can be used to measure district success and performance. The obvious ones are state-mandated reports that focus on metrics related to test scores and spending. The proliferation of data available to school districts clearly provides an opportunity to use analytics and dashboards to measure and monitor performance. In addition, many school districts are now starting to use operational or performance audits to measure efficiency and effectiveness.

INDICATORS OF DISTRICT PERFORMANCE

While no two districts are alike, there are a number of common questions or indicators that can provide insight into how a district is performing on a more global level. Being able to do a "quick" assessment or "bird's eye view" of how a district is doing is valuable to any CEO or superintendent. These indicators, along with others, constantly shape district improvement. They can be classified into six broad areas (Proviso, 2014; Schilling, 2015):

• Administrative leadership
• School board leadership
• Human resource management
• Teaching and learning
• Financial stability and sustainability
• Student-centric archetype

These are high-level organizational areas that promote and/or lay the foundation for establishing a positive district climate. District culture and oversight can trickle down and affect how individual schools and teachers function. While district success does not guarantee school improvement, it is important. When there is a shared vision among staff, and teachers are actively involved, improvements will be more successful.

Just like teachers' evaluations, district performance should not be solely based on test scores or arbitrary standards nor should it be unnecessarily complex. The challenge is creating a set of indicators that are good predictors of performance as well as simple to use. These indicators should be seen as a

Textbox 8.1. Correlating District Performance Areas with Superintendent Core Competencies

Performance Area	Superintendent Core Competencies											
	1	2	3	4	5	6	7	8	9	10	11	12
Administrative Leadership	X	X			X	X	X	X		X		X
School Board Leadership	X	X			X	X	X	X		X		
Human Resource Management		X		X			X	X				
Teaching and Learning		X	X		X	X		X	X		X	X
Financial Stability and Sustainability		X		X				X				
Student-Centric Archetype		X	X	X	X	X		X	X			X

starting, not an ending, point (Schilling, 2015). Superintendents can use these indicators as a self-assessment tool as to how their districts are doing with regard to oversight and management. The indicators can also be correlated to the core competencies for superintendents (School Community Councils, SCC) as discussed in chapter 2 (see textbox 8.1).

Administrative Leadership (refer to chapter 2; SCC 1, 2, 5, 6, 7, 8, 10, 12)

There are those that would argue that the most important thing a superintendent can do is to hire the very best administrators and then make sure they have the resources they need to get the job done. Stability in the administrative team is also crucial. To effectively implement change in a school or district there needs to be continuity. Following are some key indicators of administrative leadership:

- There is evidence of high-performing employees in every leadership position.
- The appraisal of staff is effective and performance-driven.
- There is low staff turnover.
- The administrative team fosters a positive work environment.
- Internal and external communications are clear and accurate.

- There is a good working relationship with the news media.
- Decisions are made in the best interests of students.
- Financial timelines and procedures are followed.
- There is evidence of short- and long-term planning.
- School improvement plans (SIPs) are consistent with the strategic plan of the district.
- There is compliance with the law as well as board policy.

School Board Leadership (refer to chapter 2; SCC 1, 2, 5, 6, 7, 8, 10)

Whereas superintendents implement and enforce policy, school boards set it. The balance between the board and superintendent is crucial to a successful district. Too much micromanagement and the district falters. Too little board involvement and there are no checks and balances. A healthy board/superintendent relationship ensures that all stakeholders are represented in decisions the district makes. Following are some key indicators of school board leadership:

- Board members understand and adhere to their governance role and ethical responsibilities.
- The board has the confidence and trust of voters, parents, employees, and other stakeholders.
- Board members promote the interests of schools in the communities they serve and act as a catalyst for community participation and involvement in school activities.
- Decisions are made in the best interest of students, staff, and taxpayers.
- The board monitors the accuracy and timeliness of financial and HR information.
- School facilities are attractive, safe, well-maintained, and appropriately equipped to meet educational needs (i.e., capital improvement plan).

Human Resource Management (refer to chapter 2; SCC 2, 4, 7, 8)

Not all school districts have the same level of sophistication when it comes to human resource management. For some, human resources is still basically a personnel function. For others it is all-encompassing. Since as much as 85 percent of a district's budget is for salaries and benefits, managing personnel is a high priority. Following are some key indicators of human resource management:

- There is evidence of ongoing positive and constructive communication between staff and management.
- The district has implemented or agreed to fiscally responsible compensation plans.

- The district maintains an accountability system for all staff (i.e., position control).
- There are accurate and timely enrollment projections for estimating staffing needs.
- Where appropriate, there is accurate and timely sectioning of classes based on adopted parameters.
- There are accurate and timely staffing projections.
- The district utilizes "best practices" in the recruitment, hiring, training, evaluation, and retention of personnel.

Teaching and Learning (refer to chapter 2; SCC 2, 3, 5, 6, 8, 9, 11, 12)

Teaching and learning is the core function of any school district. It includes more than just the classroom, however. It includes the opportunities given students, the way in which they are managed, and the training provided to staff. Since the passage of NCLB, addressing the needs of all disaggregated groups has also been a key consideration. Following are some key indicators of teaching and learning:

- There is evidence of continuous progress toward achieving mandated academic proficiency goals for all groups of students.
- Teachers utilize "best practices" based on data analysis and research.
- Key metrics such as graduation rates, truancy, and dropout rates are monitored.
- Disciplinary data are monitored for frequency and fairness.
- Extra/cocurricular offerings meet the needs of all students.
- There are procedures for implementing and assessing new programs, classes, etc.
- There is an effective, collaborative professional development program for staff.
- Teachers are included in decisions affecting classroom management and teaching.
- Resources are used efficiently and effectively to promote teaching and learning.
- The financial plan reflects instructional needs.

Financial Stability and Sustainability (refer to chapter 2; SCC 2, 4, 8)

The research on change says that without adequate resources either the change will not happen or will be very slow to occur. Financial information needs to be both timely and accurate, and communicated to all stakeholders. Mistrust often develops when finances are not transparent. Following are some key indicators of financial stability and sustainability:

- The district has financial recognition status from the state department of education.
- Financial information is accurate, consistent, and timely.
- An annual financial plan is completed which contains historic, current, and projected financial information.
- The district projects short- or long-term borrowing needs.
- The district communicates and fosters public understanding of its financial condition and requirements (i.e., makes financial plans, budgets, projections, etc. available on the Web).
- The district annually balances its budget.
- Compensation and benefit packages are competitive within the available resources of the district.
- The district has sustainable technology, capital improvement, and facilities plans.
- The district meets all local, state, and federal legal guidelines for fiscal operations.
- There is continuity in financial leadership.

Student-Centric Archetype (refer to chapter 2; SCC 2, 3, 4, 5, 6, 8, 9, 12)

The student-centric archetype is a model for focusing on student needs. It is a pragmatic approach that emphasizes research, best practices, efficiency, and effectiveness. Following are some key indicators of the student-centric archetype:

- Staffing allocations are logical, based on best practice, and are sustainable.
- The first priority in budgeting other than meeting legal requirements is the staffing of classroom teachers and the operating budgets which support their instruction.
- Adequate funds are allocated to meet the basic needs of each school.
- Funds are allocated to promote "grass roots" instructional improvement by teachers.
- Core and non-core functions are reviewed annually for efficiencies and effectiveness.
- Programs are continuously evaluated using a value-added approach.
- New programs or services will not be approved unless they are consistent with the strategic plan, the benefits clearly justify costs, and provisions are made for staff development and program evaluation.
- Programs or services will not be retained unless they continue to make an optimal contribution to the mission and the benefits continue to justify the costs.
- Instructional improvements, including technology, are planned for in the budget process.

OPERATIONAL AND PERFORMANCE AUDITS

A recent trend in organization efficiency and effectiveness is the use of operational and performance audits. Unlike traditional fiscal or compliance audits, these audits are performed to look for efficiencies as well as effectiveness in both core and non-core operations. An operational audit might assess the entire organization as a whole or a single operating department within a school district such as the transportation department. A performance audit might examine the effectiveness of federal grants on increasing achievement for at-risk students.

The key to a successful operational audit is to model sustainable best practices. School district performance audits focus on operational areas such as administration, transportation, plant operations, and food service and are designed to determine whether a school district is managing its resources in an effective, economical, and efficient manner. These audits provide school districts and the public with information on the use of public monies and identify best practices or make recommendations to the school districts to improve operations.

Depending on the size of the district, operational audits may be conducted by internal or external staff. The very largest districts may have an internal auditing department that does operational and management reviews in addition to compliance monitoring. Districts may also choose to employ an outside consulting firm to complete an operational audit. The advantage of using an outside firm is that they may not only have special expertise, they may have already accumulated data and/or information about best practices from which to gauge efficiency and effectiveness.

Performance audits and reviews ideally include a review of how dollars were spent in the classroom and whether it was effective. Some states, such as Oklahoma and Virginia, have state school performance review programs. The purpose of Oklahoma's School Performance Review (OSPR) Program is to develop findings, commendations, and recommendations for individual school districts regarding: 1) containing costs; 2) improving management strategies; and 3) promoting better education for Oklahoma children (Oklahoma Office of Educational Quality and Accountability, 2016).

Virginia has accumulated eight pages of school efficiency review best practices that cover a complete range of models from administrative effectiveness to teaching and learning. According to their Web site, the efficiency reviews that have been conducted since 2005 have resulted in annual savings of over $42 million (Virginia Department of Planning and Budget, 2016). Since August 2015, DPB reports that 91 percent of the recommendations from the reviews have been implemented by the districts involved.

ANALYTICS

During the past ten years the amount of data available to school districts has rapidly increased. This not only allows districts to benchmark internally but externally. Most schools have computerized their operations through the use of transactional software. Transactional software just records data and reports them. While districts still use transactional software, the trend is to move to analytical software.

Analytics has been heavily used in private industry for years for multiple reasons. Understanding consumer trends is key to sales and production. In education, it is a relatively new phenomenon. With the passage of No Child Left Behind (NCLB), data along with analytics suddenly became king. NCLB required districts to disaggregate data to see how various groups of students were performing. This led to local, state, and federal discussions on the discrepancies in student performance between various groups.

In the past, school districts have used two types of analytical tools to simply manipulate data to view trends and create projections. The first were simply spreadsheet programs that were created at the district level. A snapshot of the data was taken and analyzed. These types of programs required users to be not only proficient is using the programs but also have the time to create them.

The second type of analytical tools was data warehousing programs. Data warehousing programs allowed data to be consolidated from many different sources, such as student, finance, and testing programs, and then analyzed. In many cases those tools were expensive and difficult to use. It was not a good solution for smaller school districts.

In addition to spreadsheet and data warehousing solutions, there are now both public and private domain software to analyze a myriad of data. In fact, the problem is not how much data there are but getting them and organizing them in a meaningful way. Many states have Web sites where anyone willing to spend a little time can retrieve both information on their school district as well as comparative data on other school districts. In additional, third-party vendors have developed their own analytics for rating schools.

On the private side, a number of companies have sprung up that offer data analysis in a much simpler form. They access both district and public databases where information is stored. They allow the user to manipulate and analyze data and also present it in such a way that it can be used to communicate information to staff, the board, and the public.

Chief executive officers are well aware of the power of data. It used to be that he who had the data had the power. Since so much data are public now, it is not a matter of whether you have the data, but whether you can analyze it.

Furthermore, while the educational community can analyze test scores per se, it is only beginning to understand the relationships between teacher quality, money, and student performance/outcomes.

The current buzzwords for using analytics to report data are dashboards and infographics. Dashboards got their name from the dashboard of an automobile. When you look at a car's dashboard you immediately get feedback on how fast you're going, if the oil pressure is correct, if your lights are on, and so forth. In other words, it provides a snapshot of how your car is running.

Infographics, on the other hand, are similar to dashboard data except they are visual representations of facts, events, or numbers. Often, infographics are also interactive. For example, as you move your cursor over a pie chart representing how money is spent in a school district, there may be pop-up boxes that describe in detail the expenses. Both digital dashboards and infographics have their place in a school district. Figure 8.1 is an example of a simple dashboard to convey the status of operating reserves in a district.

As a superintendent, dashboards can be used for a number of purposes. There are a number of key considerations when a district decides to use dashboards such as:

1. What type of dashboard reports?
2. Who is the audience?
3. What data will you report?
4. What will be the data characteristics?

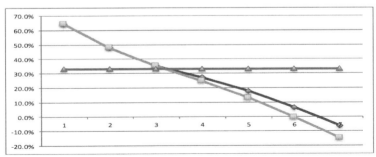

District Financial Dashboard - Operating Fund Reserves

	2013	2014	2015	2016	2017	2018	2019
Current	64.4%	47.8%	35.2%	27.3%	17.8%	6.4%	-6.2%
Base	64.4%	47.8%	35.2%	24.7%	13.1%	-0.3%	-14.9%
Board Goal	33.0%	33.0%	33.0%	33.0%	33.0%	33.0%	33.0%

Figure 8.1. Example of a simple dashboard report to communicate decreasing operating reserves.

Dashboards can be used to both inform and empower. They can inform the board, staff, parents, community members, realtors, prospective families or businesses, and other stakeholders. They can also be used to empower the management team to make good decisions.

If you have operational dashboards, determine which ones would be helpful to board members. Data-driven decision-making in schools is a relatively new occurrence in education compared to the private sector. It enhances the ability of schools and school districts to make data-driven changes and decisions. For example, it assists in identifying at-risk students, making evaluations, communicating results to parents, identifying in real-time where interventions can take place, and assisting in the allocation of human and financial resources.

In the not-too-distant future, individual student achievement will be correlated with human resource and financial data. Superintendents will be able to see if resources are being utilized efficiently and effectively. These types of reports (dashboards) are beginning to be incorporated into student, finance, and human resource software systems available to K–12 school systems.

For schools and school districts, dashboards are the business intelligence for education. They provide real-time metrics and benchmarks, measure direct impact, and provide performance monitoring. For purposes of dashboard reporting, a performance metric is a measure of the school's activities and performance. These would include demographic, finance, human resources, and instructional and operational activities of the organization. Just the mere fact of having metrics and reviewing them drives change. It empowers schools, their administrative staffs, and their board members to make changes that are impactful and not merely cosmetic.

To support change, accurate data need to be available to the right people in the right format. They also need to be transparent to all stakeholders. That is one of the primary benefits of routinely collecting, analyzing, and sharing data. The new dimensions of analytics are business intelligence, metrics, and performance.

The new dimensions are being used by administrators to discover trends, create projections, and communicate their impact to stakeholders. As a superintendent, consider who will use the dashboards, what information will be displayed, and how the information will be communicated. Are they for internal or external use? Are the data something that you can release to the public? Are you going to place the dashboards on the Web?

How can dashboards be used in a district's planning process? One example is to use them to tell a story of where your district has been, where it is, and where it is going. In the fall of each year, schedule dashboard reports of all the major areas in the school district.

- September—Finance
- October—Instruction
- November—Human Resources
- December—Demographic

ANALYTICS, CHANGE, AND PERFORMANCE

Ultimately, the purpose of performance indicators, operational audits, and analytics is not just to report to stakeholders but to determine how to improve performance. So where does an organization start? How does an organization know what needs to be changed first? How does the organization set priorities and determine urgency? For many school districts, the process of prioritizing opportunities is an arduous process. Some organizations use elaborate and protracted processes such as strategic planning. The problem with a protracted approach is that by the time needs are identified and prioritized, their urgency may have altered. Besides prioritizing opportunities, an organization must distinguish between the urgency of the needs identified and its willingness to execute the change, especially when the need for the change is critical.

School organizations often fall into the trap of feeling that "everything is important." Give a group a survey like a Likert scale where everything can be ranked important and often you will get just that—a list where everything is important and there is no distinction between the urgency of the items. Knowing that opportunities need to be seized in a timely manner means that school systems need mechanisms or strategies to prioritize the urgency of their needs. That is why analytics and performance indicators are important. There is an optimum time for any change.

There is a significant difference between systemic changes implemented by a school district and those implemented by the school or department. School districts tend to use systemic changes because they are cost-effective and efficient. They are not, however, necessarily the most effective with respect to changing academic performance or changing school culture and climate.

For effective and lasting changes to occur at the building, department, or grade levels, the achievement and culture of each unit must be respected. Unfortunately, while change that is implemented on an individual building basis can be more impactful, it can also be more expensive in terms of staff time and financial resources. Think of choosing a new textbook. Simply choosing a new book on a district-wide basis can be quick and cost effective. Doing so on a building-by-building basis would involve a much larger commitment of time, staff, and resources—especially if different textbooks were chosen at different schools.

Aside from change that is implemented to be compliant with state or federal laws, there are two variables to note—the urgency and efficacy of the change. If we created a grid with urgency on one side and resource demand on the other, where would each change lie? Which changes are high priority but present the greatest challenges with regard to procuring resources? Which changes require few resources to execute? Which changes in resource alignment and allocation need to take place to ensure success? Are there changes which are just "too big"?

Likewise, district performance should be monitored along similar parameters. Knowing what to monitor, when to measure it, how to interpret the results, and what, if any, changes need to be made is crucial. No one person can pull all that off by themselves. To be successful, organizations need an internal network to collect data, interpret them, and identify and implement change.

Figure 8.2 shows the relationship between the urgency and the readiness for change. Whereas urgency is simply a timing issue, readiness means that

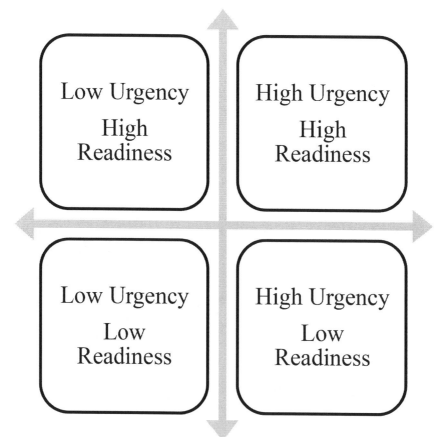

Figure 8.2. The relationship between the urgency and readiness for change.

staff are ready, resources have been procured, and a plan has been developed. Urgency may be a result of a government mandate, pressure to increase student performance, projections of financial distress, or a failing facility. What is important is to create a performance monitoring system that picks up deviations in performance before they adversely impact the organization. That may include performance indicators, audits, and analytics.

SUMMARY

One of the difficulties for anyone using data is the tendency to "fail to see the forest for the trees." All levels of management need some simple strategic tools to ascertain how their business is doing. Gauging some global performance indicators is a quick way for superintendents to determine how the district they serve is doing.

There are six broad areas that can be monitored to determine district performance. They are:

- Administrative leadership
- School board leadership
- Human resource management
- Teaching and learning
- Financial stability and sustainability
- Student-centric archetype

These areas are by no means mutually exclusive nor are they meant to be all-inclusive. They are a starting point. The performance indicators provided for these areas will always have to be modified based on the unique attributes of a particular school or district.

Operational and performance audits are viable strategies for establishing efficiencies and gauging the effectiveness of a school district. They can include both instructional and noninstructional areas such as transportation, buildings and grounds, and food service. Operational and performance audits rely heavily on "best practice" models in various areas.

Analytics and dashboards offer a district the means to gather intelligence, forecast, collaborate, and manage information. They allow for the development of custom datasets and analytics. They can be graphical representations of data to better communicate it to stakeholders (infographics) or dashboards which organize data from various sources.

The idea that "data is king" still has merit. The difference between now and ten years ago, however, is that there is no shortage of data. The challenge now is to mine the information to find relationships that will help school districts improve.

CASE STUDY

For the past five years you have been the superintendent of a small semirural school district. Board/superintendent relations were excellent and the district worked collaboratively to increase student performance while addressing some issues with truancy. You've decided to make a move to a larger suburban district. The district covers five different communities, is approximately 45 percent low-income, and has struggled to meet state academic standards.

Upon taking your new position, you discover that not everything is as it appeared. There are multiple issues which need to be addressed and the school board is divided on many of them. You decide you need to do a quick assessment of the district so you use the indicators of school district performance. Unfortunately, the results are not good. There is much work to be done. For example, you find that:

- The current financial plan is unsustainable.
- There hasn't been a self-evaluation of the board for years.
- There is an ongoing backlog of grievances from the union.
- The board struggles with prioritizing needs. There are more "wants" than resources.
- There appears to be little interest by the community in participating in programs to get families involved in the school.
- The district is not meeting its academic proficiency goals.
- There is no accurate accountability for the number of staff allocated.
- Evaluations have not been consistently completed on all administrators.
- School budgets are set with little or no input from principals and teachers.
- It appears that there is communication outside the chain of command that causes confusion and blurs the line of authority between the board and superintendent.
- There is a lack of evidence that resources are being used efficiently and effectively to promote teaching and learning.

Based on this information 1) how would you go about communicating your findings to the board and other stakeholders? 2) How would you develop a plan to address these concerns? 3) How would you go about ensuring that everyone is involved in the process? 4) Outline a plan to evaluate how successful the plan was in addressing the concerns.

EXERCISES AND DISCUSSION QUESTIONS

1. How would you use the indicators of district performance as a superintendent? Do you believe there is merit in using them with other stakeholders such as the board?

2. You've decided to have a performance audit on the use of federal funds to see if they are effectively being utilized. How would you communicate to staff that you are having the performance audit performed? What would you tell staff with regard to the goals of the audit?
3. Describe how you would utilize analytics as part of an accountability program for the performance of your school district team.
4. Review the list of indicators of district performance. Are there any key indicators that aren't on the list? If so, what are they and why are they important?
5. What key metrics do you believe a school district should monitor and share with its staff?
6. Waters, Marzano, and McNulty (2003) outlined twenty-one leadership practices that were required for first- or second-order change to take place. What they found is that for first-order change to take place there had to be a sense of collaboration, well-being, and solidarity among staff. Second-order change, however, required that staff develop a shared vision. How can district performance indicators and metrics be used to foster first- and second-order change?
7. What key metrics do you believe a school district should monitor and share with the community on the Web?

REFERENCES

Oklahoma Office of Educational Quality and Accountability. (2016). *Oklahoma School Performance Review*. Retrieved from https://www.ok.gov/oeqa/Oklahoma_School_Performance_Review/.

Proviso Township High School District 209 Financial Oversight Panel (2014, May 30). Proviso Township High School District transition benchmarks. Retrieved from http://www.pths209.org/assets/1/7/Proviso_Transition_Benchmarks.pdf.

Schilling, C. (2015). *Trends in American education*. Education Business Leadership Course, Melbourne, Australia.

Virginia Department of Planning and Budget. (2016). *Matrix of school review best practice recommendations and best practice models*. Retrieved from http://www.dpb.virginia.gov/school/Matrix.cfm.

Waters, T., Marzano, R. J., & McNulty, B. (2003). *Balanced leadership: What 30 years of research tells us about the effect of leadership on student achievement.* McREL (Mid-continent Research for Education and Learning).

Appendix A

School Leadership Survey

School Leadership Survey

Principal: _____   Superintendent: _____   Graduate School Leadership Student _____

Thank you for taking the time to complete this survey. The purpose of this survey is to collect data from school leaders to gain a better understanding of the core competencies desired for the position. The survey should take you no more than 5-10 minutes to complete. Our hope is that this data will help plan appropriate school leadership programs. You can elect to skip any items you wish or to discontinue the survey at any time. Your name is not attached to your survey responses.

Instructions: Please rate each core competency in regards to the degree of importance for a school superintendent (0= no importance and 5= very important).

Rating	Core Competencies	Description
_____	1. Working with board members	Collaborating and working with the school district board members.
_____	2. Understanding school law	Understanding legal and laws impacting school district leadership and operations.
_____	3. Being an instructional leader	Being a proactive and involved leader in improving school district instruction.
_____	4. Managing resources	Managing financial, facility, and human resources and regulations.
_____	5. Leading and motivating	Leading and motivating staff for improved performance in achieving school initiatives.
_____	6. Managing school change	Leading and managing school change and improvements.
_____	7. Communicating	Communicating to school district staff and stakeholders.
_____	8. Setting goals	Developing and setting educational goals
_____	9. Understanding school data	Interpreting and using school data and assessment information.
_____	10. Building community relations	Developing and working with school community members, parents, etc.
_____	11. Understanding diverse learning	Providing effective instruction for diverse students
_____	12. Building Collaboration	Building collaboration and teamwork.

Please write other important competencies or other comments below or on back of this page.

Figure A.1.

Appendix B

Sample Professional Learning and Growth Plans

Superintendent

Date: _____	Name: _____
District: _____	Position: Superintendent
	Evaluator: Board of Education
Performance Rating: _____	

ELCC - 3 and PSEL - 4, 10				
Goal: Improve student performance				
Action Steps	*Time*	*Resources*	*Person*	*Evidence*

A. Identify district student performance goals and indicators to measure them for the district, each school and each student sub-group.
  1. Analyze student test data and determine goals for the district, each school, and each student sub-group.
  2. Select indicators that will measure student performance in the district, at each school and for each sub-group.
B. Identify research-based instructional strategies.
  1. Direct assistant superintendent to identify research-based instructional strategies to be used by all teachers in classrooms.
  2. Direct assistant superintendent to develop professional learning and growth plan for principals and teachers.
	Summer	Allocate budget for stipends to pay district leadership team for work over the summer	Superintendent and Board of Education with assistance from other district and school leaders	1. Student performance data reported at spring board meeting
				
				2. Student performance learning goals, curriculum plans, instructional resources presented at subsequent board meetings

Date: _____   Name: _____

District: _____   Position: _____

School: _____   Evaluator: <u>Superintendent or designee</u>

Performance Rating: _____

Goal: Research, organize and prepare a bargaining plan for noncertified nonunion staff to present to the Superintendent and Board of Education ELCC - 2,5 and PSEL - 2, 7, 9				
Action Steps	*Time*	*Resources*	*Person*	*Evidence*

A. Create an organizational plan that will develop a culture which values an ethical and transparent negotiation process.
  1. Work with staff leadership to identify terms for the negotiation team to consider.
  2. Write a plan of action for the negotiation process.
  3. Identify needed resources for the process.
 	
B. Review the plan with district and school leaders.
  1. Discuss strategies and negotiation terms and procedures.
  2. Edit and make changes as needed.
  3. Present plan to the Board of Education in closed session.
  4. Seek approval for process.
	Spring	Allocate time for district/ school leaders and team members to work on the plan.	District Admin	1. Staff climate survey and work data from previous year reported to District, School and Members.
				
				2. Staff performance goals and evaluations.
				
				3. Staff Professional Learning and Growth Plans.

Date: _____	Name: _____
District: _____	Position: Principal
School: _____	Evaluator: Superintendent or designee

Performance Rating: _____

Goal: Improve student performance and teacher effectiveness ELCC - 2, 3 and PSEL - 4, 6, 7				
Action Steps	*Time*	*Resources*	*Person*	*Evidence*
A. Develop a School Leadership Team. 　1. Select teacher leaders who are representative of school stakeholders to serve on the School Leadership Team. 　2. Examine indicator data to identify school faculty needs for learning and growth 　3. Facilitate preparation of the School Professional Learning and Growth Plan for faculty and staff.	Spring	Allocate funds to pay district school leaders, team members for work over the summer	Principal	1. Student performance data from last school year reported at spring board meeting. 2. Student performance goals for new school year presented at spring board meeting.
B. Create organizational processes and procedures that will develop a culture which values continuous improvement and lifelong learning. 　1. Work with school leadership team to schedule time during school year for teacher training in teaming. 　2. Work with school leadership team to develop collaborative and interdisciplinary teams. C. Develop professional learning and growth culture in the school. 　1. Coach and mentor teacher leaders. 　2. Train teachers in research-based instructional strategies.	School year	Money for release time for school leaders, team to meet, train, and coach and mentor teachers during the school day		3. School Professional Learning and Growth Plan. 4. Inter-disciplinary team agendas, minutes, recommendations for next meeting.

Date: _____   Name: _____

District: _____   Position: Assistant Principal

School: _____   Evaluator: Principal

Performance Rating: _____

Goal: Promote a positive school culture and climate ELCC - 2, 4 and PSEL - 1, 3, 6, 9				
Action Steps	*Time*	*Resources*	*Person*	*Evidence*
A. Create a school wide plan that will develop a culture which values an ethical and transparent process for student discipline. 　1. Develop a School Discipline Team. 　2. Seek teacher leaders who are representative of school stakeholders to serve on the team. 　3. Seek parents to participate on the team. 　4. Examine indicator data to identify needs for improved student discipline and lower referral rates.	Fall	Allocate time for school leaders & team members to work on the plan.	Assistant Principal	1. Staff climate survey and discipline referral data from previous years. 2. Student survey about school-wide discipline procedures. 3. Parent survey about school-wide discipline procedures.
B. Create an organizational plan that will develop a discipline code and a guide for faculty and staff. 　1. Work with team to identify best practices in promoting positive student behavior. 　2. Write a proposed discipline code. 　3. Identify needed resources for the implementation process. 　4. Seek faculty, staff, and student input and approval of the school-wide code.	Fall			1. Team meeting minutes showing writing progress and discussions. 2. Draft plan

Figure B.1.

Appendix C

The following is a summary of the 2015 Professional Standards for Educational Leaders (PSEL), formerly known as the ISLLC Standards.

STANDARD 1. Mission, Vision, and Core Values
Effective educational leaders develop, advocate, and enact a shared mission, vision, and core values of high-quality education and academic success and well-being of *each* student.

STANDARD 2. Ethics and Professional Norms
Effective educational leaders act ethically and according to professional norms to promote *each* student's academic success and well-being.

STANDARD 3. Equity and Cultural Responsiveness
Effective educational leaders strive for equity of educational opportunity and culturally responsive practices to promote *each* student's academic success and well-being.

STANDARD 4. Curriculum, Instruction, and Assessment
Effective educational leaders develop and support intellectually rigorous and coherent systems of curriculum, instruction, and assessment to promote *each* student's academic success and well-being.

STANDARD 5. Community of Care and Support for Students
Effective educational leaders cultivate an inclusive, caring, and supportive school community that promotes the academic success and well-being of *each* student.

STANDARD 6. Professional Capacity of School Personnel
Effective educational leaders develop the professional capacity and practice of school personnel to promote *each* student's academic success and well-being.

STANDARD 7. Professional Community for Teachers and Staff
Effective educational leaders foster a professional community of teachers and other professional staff to promote *each* student's academic success and well-being.

STANDARD 8. Meaningful Engagement of Families and Community
Effective educational leaders engage families and the community in meaningful, reciprocal, and mutually beneficial ways to promote *each* student's academic success and well-being.

STANDARD 9. Operations and Management
Effective educational leaders manage school operations and resources to promote *each* student's academic success and well-being.

STANDARD 10. School Improvement
Effective educational leaders act as agents of continuous improvement to promote *each* student's academic success and well-being.

Council of Chief States School Officers, http://www.ccsso.org

Index

90/90/90 schools study, 88

AASA. *See* The School Superintendents Association (formerly American Association of School Administrators)
American Recovery and Reinvestment Act (2009), 10
analytical software, 140; analytics (as a practice), 115–16, 133–34, 140–43, 145, 147
A Nation At Risk, 6, 8, 10, 38

bargaining power, 5
Bell, Terrel, 6
benchmark, 117, 122, 133, 140, 142, 147
best instructional practices, 22
Brierton, Jeffrey T., 7, 157
Brown v. Board of Education (1954), 58–59
Bush, George W., 8
business intelligence, 142
buy-in, 80
buzzwords, 141

CAEP (Council for the Accreditation of Educator Preparation), 42
centralization, 3

change leadership, 25, 43–44, 52
coaching/mentoring relationship, 79–83
cocurricular, 137
"co-labor," 30
collaborative, 20, 30, 32, 34, 39, 40, 44, 48–49, 71, 80, 83, 85, 88, 93, 100, 109, 114, 122, 137, 146
collective bargaining, 4–5, 158
commingling, 23
Common Core State Standards (Common Core), 9–10, 59, 70, 73, 128
continuous participation theory, 63–65
core competencies, 37, 103–4; of school leaders, 17–32; of superintendents, 40–48, 52
Council of Chief State School Officers (CCSSO), 9, 156
culture-oriented leadership, 47

Danielson Framework for Teaching, 11
dashboards, 134, 141–42, 145
databases, 140
data-driven, 28, 78, 82, 123, 142
"data is king," 145
datasets, 145
data warehousing programs, 140
decision-making, 12, 24, 28 40, 66, 120, 142
demotivating factor of favoritism, 109

Department of Defense Education
    Activity (DoDEA), 10
digital natives, 27
DiPaola, Michael F., 13, 48
disaggregate, 137, 140
dissatisfaction theory, 63–64, 75
downsizing, 126
drop-ins, 83
dropout rates, 137
DuFour, Richard, 31

Educational Leadership Constituent
    Council (ELCC), 1, 17, 37, 41–42,
    57, 83, 86, 90, 93, 111, 133
Education for All Handicapped Children
    Act of 1975 (EHCA), 58–59, 73
effective superintendent, 10, 12–13,
    21–29, 30–31, 40, 51
Elementary and Secondary Education
    Act of 1965 (ESEA) amended in
    2011, 8, 58–59, 73
English language arts/literacy (ELA), 9
entry-level, 10
Every Student Succeeds Act of 2015
    (ESSA), 11–12, 59, 70, 73
evidence-based, 10, 68

fast track, 24
feedback, 68, 77–83, 85, 88, 91, 105–7,
    141
fiduciary, 113
first-order change, 147
follow-up interviews, 41
forerunner, 2
four-domain model, 11
Freedom of Information Act (FOIA), 24
functionally illiterate, 7
fusion leadership, 48, 50–52

global marketplace, 6, 33
grade-level assessments, 83
Great Depression, 4

higher-order thinking skills, 10
high-level curriculum, 59

high-performing school organization, 28
high-poverty districts, 71, 88
high-stakes accountability, 19, 33
high-stakes testing environment, 28, 30,
    80
Holmes, Oliver Wendell, 101

Illinois Association of School Business
    Officials (IASBO), 158
Illinois State Board of Education
    Licensure Board Peer Review Panels,
    157
Individuals with Disabilities Education
    Act of 1997 (IDEA), 73
infographics, 141, 145
Interstate School Leaders Licensure
    Consortium (ISLLC), 155

Jefferson, Thomas, 2
job-embedded, 82

key performance indicators (KPIs), 99
King, Dr. Martin Luther, Jr., 25, 31
knowledge delivery system, 22
Kouzes, James, 43

laser-beam focus, 50
leader-focused, 86
Leadership Practices Inventory (LPI),
    43
learning leader, 37–38, 40, 52–53
learning organizations, 47–49
legacy dogma, 33
level-five leader, 32
life-long learning, 7
Likert scale, 43, 143
local educational agencies (LEAs), 8
loose coupling, 38

macro-level decisions, 70
marginal leader, 87–88
Massachusetts Bay Colony, 2
McKinney-Vento Homeless Assistance
    Act, 73–74
merit pay, 7

meta-analysis, 87

metrics, 28, 94, 99, 134, 137, 142. *See also* key performance indicators (KPIs)

Mid-Continent Research for Education and Learning (McREL), 87, 147

mission statement, 96–98

modified clinical supervision model, 84

moral leadership, 108

multipliers, 24

multi-rater feedback, 107

National Commission on Excellence in Education, 6, 7

National Governors Association Center (NGA), 9

National School Boards Association (NSBA), 59, 71, 72

NCATE (National Council for Accreditation of Teacher Education), 42

needs assessment, 27

"new, flat world," 32, 33

No Child Left Behind Act of 2001 (NCLB), 8–9, 11, 59, 73

noncontractual policies, 19,

non-core functions, 117, 128–29, 138

nonnegotiables, 35, 80, 85

nonpolitical, 63

nonrandom, 43

one-size-fits-all, 72, 78

on-site, 84

open-ended, 41

open narrative evaluation, 107

organized labor movement, 5

out-perform, 88

outsource, 117

overseer, 2

oversight, 57–59, 73, 113, 117, 128, 134–35

overuse, 27

parochial, 3

pass/fail grade, 119

payback period, 123

performance management plan, 78, 82, 100

performance metric, 94, 99, 100–1, 142

pilot study, 118–19

plenary, 58

policymaking, 34, 65, 67

pop-up boxes, 141

Posner, Barry, 43

post-narrative, 84

postsecondary education, 72

poverty-concentrated, 72

power candidate, 65

prestige candidate, 65

proactive leader, 21, 108

professional development, 38, 78–79, 82, 90–93, 104–6, 109, 118, 124–25, 137

professional learning community (PLC), 35,39, 44, 47–48, 53, 91

professional learning team model, 32,

Professional Standards for Educational Leaders, 2015 (PSEL) [formerly ISLLC], 1, 17, 37, 40–42, 57, 77, 83, 86, 90–92, 93, 111, 133, 155

public choice theory, 63, 65, 75

quasi-market, 51

Race to the Top, 10

rational choice background, 65

reactive leader, 108

redrawing, 67

reformers, 11, 48

remediation, 9

renegotiated, 11

repurpose, 115, 118, 123, 128

research-based, 84–85, 88–90, 92, 128

roadblock, 79

road map, 96

rubrics, 11, 80

Schilling, Craig A., 109, 120, 122, 126, 134–35, 158

school factors, 88

school improvement grant(s), 12
school improvement plans (SIPs), 71, 85, 90, 96, 124, 133, 136
The School Superintendents Association (formerly American Association of School Administrators), 18, 42, 90
school-wide, 80, 93
scorecards, 99
self-assessment, 84, 135
self-report, 43
semiautonomous, 5
semirural, 146
servant leadership, 12, 20, 30, 108
shared decision-making model, 12
shared leadership, 4, 22
short-lived, 44
silos, 51
simplest test, 7
single-focus, 66
skill-driven curriculums, 21
SMART (specific, measurable, attainable, realistic, and timely), 99; goals, 99
social-emotional, 29
Soviet satellite Sputnik in 1957, 8
spreadsheet programs, 140
stakeholders, 12, 20, 25–27, 31, 39. 51, 53, 90, 97–98, 100, 109, 112–13, 122, 124–26, 134, 136–37, 142–46
standards-based models, 83–84
standards-based reform, 9
standards-driven, 42
start-up business,117
state-led, 9
strategic planning committee, 27
steward, 20, 23, 38, 59, 111–12, 128
student-centric archetype, 138, 145
student-centric budgeting (SCB) model, 124, 126, 128–29
student factors, 88
subdistrict electoral boundaries, 3

subgroups,12
succession planning, 93, 101–4, 109–10
summative, 79, 81, 83–84, 105–7
superintendent as CEO, 113, 116, 134
SWOT (strengths, weaknesses, opportunities, and threats), 95–99; analysis, 95–99
systems thinking, 50–52, 52–54; as countermeasure, 51; organizational model, 50

teacher evaluation reform, 8, 10
teacher leaders, 43, 80–81, 89
teacher-scholar, 38
teacher-student performance, 85
teachers' unions, 4–6, 8, 11 19, 26, 65
Tenth Amendment to the United States Constitution, 2, 58
third-party vendors, 140
time-intensive process, 85
Tomal, Daniel R., 81, 109, 158
top-down approach, 38–40
transactional software, 140
twenty-first-century superintendent, 2, 21, 32, 51
two-track educational system, 2

value-added model, 10–11
value proposition model, 119–20
values statement, 97
Virginia, 2, 139, 147
vision statement, 27, 96–98

wake-up call, 45
watch lists, 87
Wilhite, Robert K., 157
workforce, 10
working-age, 71
world-class, 23–24, 29
worst-case scenario, 85

About the Authors

Robert K. Wilhite, EdD, is professor of leadership, the Dean of the College of Graduate Studies at Concordia University Chicago, and former chair of the Department of Leadership. He is a retired superintendent of schools, as well as an elementary, middle school, and high school principal, and an associate superintendent for curriculum and instruction. He is coauthor of several Rowman & Littlefield Education (RLE) books including *Ethics and Politics in School Leadership*; *Transforming Professional Practice: A Framework for Effective Leadership*; *Supervision and Evaluation for Learning and Growth*; *The Teacher Leader: Core Competencies and Strategies for Effective Leadership* and has made numerous presentations at conferences in areas of leadership styles and curriculum development. He also currently serves on the Illinois State Board of Education Licensure Board Peer Review Panels evaluating the design of university principal and superintendent preparation programs in Illinois.

Jeffrey T. Brierton, PhD, is associate professor of leadership at Concordia University Chicago (CUC). He is a former teacher, administrator, and high school principal, and interim superintendent who received a BA degree in political science from Elmhurst College, an MA degree in political science from Roosevelt University, an MSEd from Northern Illinois University, an EdS from National Louis University, and a PhD in American history from Loyola University. Dr. Brierton teaches leadership courses and is a university supervisor for the CUC principal internship program. He is also a retired ten-year veteran of the U.S. Army Reserve. He is coauthor of the book *Ethics and Politics in School Leadership*, published by Rowman & Littlefield.

Craig A. Schilling, EdD, is associate professor of educational leadership at Concordia University Chicago. He has been a public school administrator, systems analyst, and CEO. He has consulted with numerous school districts and has spoken and presented throughout the United States, Australia, Canada, and the Caribbean. He is a past president of the Illinois Association of School Business Officials. He has received numerous awards for his contributions to the field of school business management. He is coauthor of the books *Resource Management for School Administrators: Optimizing Fiscal, Facility, and Human Resources*; *Managing Human Resources and Collective Bargaining*; *Leading School Change: Maximizing Resources for School Improvement*; and *The Teacher Leader: Core Competencies and Strategies for Effective Leadership*, all published by Rowman & Littlefield.

Daniel R. Tomal, PhD, is distinguished professor of leadership at Concordia University Chicago and has published twenty books (several with Rowman & Littlefield) and over two hundred articles and studies. He has testified before the United States Congress and has consulted for numerous schools and organizations. He is a former school administrator, high school teacher, and corporate consultant. He has made guest appearances on many national and local television and radio shows such as CBS *This Morning*, NBC *Cover to Cover*, ABC *News*, *Les Brown*, *Joan Rivers*, *Chicago Talks*, etc.